Wildlife of Maldon

Main author: John Buchanan

Contributing team:

Simon Wood, Russell Neave, Emma Neave-Webb and Simon Patient

A celebration of the wildlife to be encountered in and around the historic Essex town of Maldon and an account of how it has been changing over the last twenty years.

Fully illustrated with photographs taken within the area

Black-tailed Godwit
(Rebecca Buchanan)

CONTENTS

Appendices:

The Estuary at dawn

INTRODUCTION

For a group of us living locally at the time, the first two decades of the 21st century has represented a period of intense wildlife watching in and around the town of Maldon. Although making occasional forays elsewhere, we focused most of our available time within walking distance of our homes. It felt great to be finding good birds and other wildlife without spending time and fuel in travelling lengthy distances by car.

It soon became apparent that the crossover between the 20th and 21st centuries was proving to be an era of significant change for local wildlife. Traditional species such as Spotted Flycatcher and Grey Partridge were being lost as breeding species, while in the meantime there have been arrivals of new colonists, such as Little Egret and a host of new invertebrates, from moths to dragonflies. Dramatic changes are also taking place in the landscape due to increasing housing development and changes in agricultural practices.

There was a previous heyday, when Red-backed Shrike bred and farmland birds flourished, but little of this period was recorded. We felt it would be regrettable if our own experiences should be lost in the same way. Two other factors have helped the project — the surge in digital photography (we all now generally carry a camera wherever we go) and the sharing of information via the internet, which has meant that sightings and knowledge can be readily and quickly shared by and amongst the wider community who birdwatch in the area.

The intent here is to capture the essence of observations between 2000 and 2020. By happy coincidence, this period has also been one of ready availability of excellent locally brewed beer, the consumption of which has played no small part in the planning of much of the activity that has gone into this book!

It is hoped that this portrait of the town's wildlife may spread awareness of how much can be found on one's doorstep and encourage others to explore and take an interest in protecting their own local environment so that the sights described can continue to be seen for generations to come.

The Prom almost covered on a high spring tide, Nov 2020

1

SETTING THE SCENE

A Maldon primer

The Essex town of Maldon is strategically sited at the head of the Blackwater estuary. It provides the most westerly navigable mooring for ships and hence has been historically important both as a site to defend against invading forces and as a trading station for goods arriving by sea and destined for Chelmsford and communities further inland.

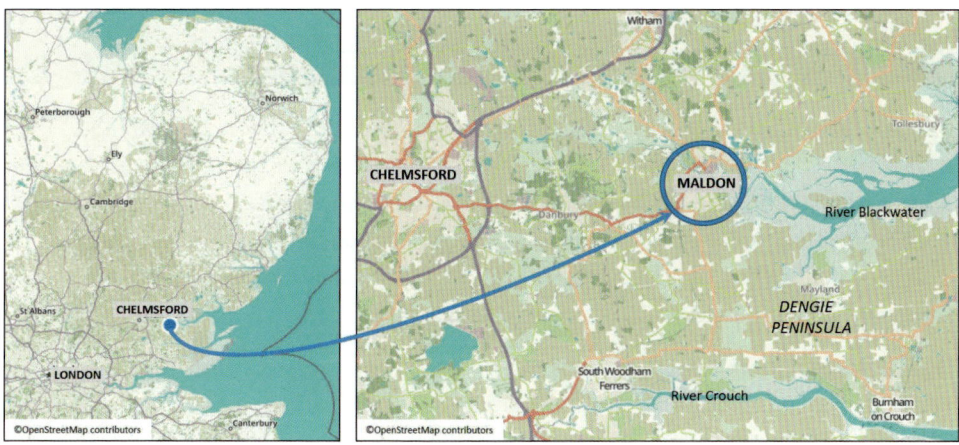

Maldon's location 11 miles east of Chelmsford (45 miles from central London)

Maldon has a long human history. Neolithic pottery fragments found during excavations around Lofts Farm by the Maldon Archaeological Group have been dated to 3500 BC. In the same general area, some evidence has been found of later Bronze and Iron Age settlements including ring ditches indicating 'round house' building styles. The Romans arrived some time after 40 AD and seem to have established a small town around the site of modern day Heybridge, using the location as a port. As the Romans departed, Saxons appeared of whom some traces have also been found, though there is generally little evidence of life during the following 'Dark Ages'.

The earliest specific reference to 'Maldon' relates to 912 AD when, according to the Anglo-Saxon Chronicles, Edward the Elder, son of Alfred the Great, made camp here

while building forts in the vicinity. A few years later it is said that he built a fortified settlement, or buhr, at Maldon, which he then used as a base while he engaged in skirmishes with Viking raiding forces. It is believed the walls of the buhr encircled what is now the top of London Road, stretching between Beeleigh Road and St Peter's Hospital. Within the 10th century, Maldon was established as a mint — a site where moneyers could issue coins.

Maldon's main historical notoriety comes from the year 991 when, at the Battle of Maldon, Byrhtnoth, Ealdorman of Essex, lost his life leading an Anglo-Saxon force against later Viking invaders. Although his troops lost the battle, they inflicted sufficient injury to these Vikings that the latter left the vicinity and turned their attentions elsewhere (for a while at least!).

↑ The River Blackwater spreading out from Maldon

→ John Doubleday's imposing statue of Ealdorman Byrhtnoth, stands proudly on the end of Maldon Prom, guarding against future invading forces

The story of this dramatic encounter was written up as a poem in Old English that has passed down to us through the centuries. This text provides the earliest known reference to wildlife in Maldon as it suggests the presence of Raven ('hremmas') and Eagle ('earn', presumably White-tailed Eagle) seeking out carrion on the battlefield.

By the time of the Domesday Book in 1086, Maldon had 54 houses and 180 townsmen. Maldon was sufficiently prominent for Henry II to award the town a Royal Charter in 1171, conferring rights to the town and defining its borders and its obligations, including the provision of a ship for the Navy.

Over later centuries, Maldon further expanded as a port with an increasing volume and variety of goods being landed at the Hythe Quay ('hythe' is derived from an Anglo Saxon word for haven). Onward transport of goods was at first all by road but then later also by water following the opening of the Chelmer and Blackwater Navigation in 1797.

The originally planned routing of the navigation via Maldon was objected to by those in the town who felt they would lose tax revenues on goods not imported directly there and so a length of canal was created to connect to the sea at nearby Heybridge instead. The community around Heybridge Basin was spawned by the resulting construction works.

The canal locks at Heybridge

Further improvement in transportation was achieved by the construction of rail links. Firstly, a branch line to Witham, opened in 1848, and then a southerly Maldon to Woodham Ferrers line that opened in 1889. With the railway, Maldon became a destination for day-trippers from London, catalysing the creation of the Promenade Park (generally known as simply the 'Prom Park'), which remains in much the same form to this day.

Moorings along the edge of the Promenade ('the Prom') were used by a fleet of 'smacks', gaff-rigged sailing vessels used for fishing and for harvesting the Blackwater oyster beds. Some of the original smacks are still to be seen during the annual Old Gaffers Rally.

Thames sailing barges moored at Maldon Hythe

Throughout this time, much of the maritime trade was carried out using flat-bottomed Thames sailing barges. Some were built at Maldon and the boatyards still carry out barge repairs and renovation work. Although their use for commercial cargoes has long ceased, a number of Thames barges have been preserved and based at Maldon where they are available for tourist trips and charter hire. They have an imposing presence on the river, especially with their iconic red-ochre-stained sails unfurled to catch the wind.

During the 20th century the town expanded and housing estates replaced orchards and farmland. Following the ill-judged findings of the Beeching Report, both railway stations were closed by 1966 and, subsequently, a bypass along with a new road bridge over the river was constructed along much of the route of the old railway, opening in 1990. (Up to this point all through vehicular traffic had to go through the centre of Maldon and across Fullbridge). As a result of gravel workings that were then flooded, there are now a variety of artificially created bodies of water in the area, including the somewhat brackish Heybridge Pits and the complex of lakes around Chigborough and Lofts Farms. Most of the lakes, as well as the canal and Chelmer and Blackwater Navigation, have been opened up for various forms of fishing.

May Water, one of the flooded gravel pits at Chigborough

The Handley Green building estate constructed on agricultural land to the south of Maldon, part of the Limebrook Park development which will deliver 1,000 more homes to the area

The combined human population of Maldon and Heybridge at the time of the 2011 National Census was around 22,400. Currently however there is major ongoing expansion in line with Maldon District Council's Local Development Plan, based around a 2014 proposal to construct 2,830 further houses.

This is being achieved primarily by the creation of two new 'garden suburbs' in areas of existing farmland — South Maldon and North Heybridge Garden Suburbs.

In the face of this period of further change, we feel it timely to document the current wildlife of Maldon, for the interest of both present and incoming residents and also to provide a historical record for future generations to reflect upon.

"The Patch"

The geographical area that has been the focus of our wildlife watching is known fondly to us as 'The Maldon Patch'. The definition arose when Russell Neave and Simon Wood were trying to decide which of their sightings could be described as 'local'. Looking at a map it became apparent that all the main localities were within three miles of Russell's house at the time, and so it was that somewhat arbitrarily they defined their 'local patch' as being all the area bounded by a circle with a radius of three miles centred on 219 Mundon Road.

MAP OF "THE PATCH" — OUR MALDON STUDY AREA

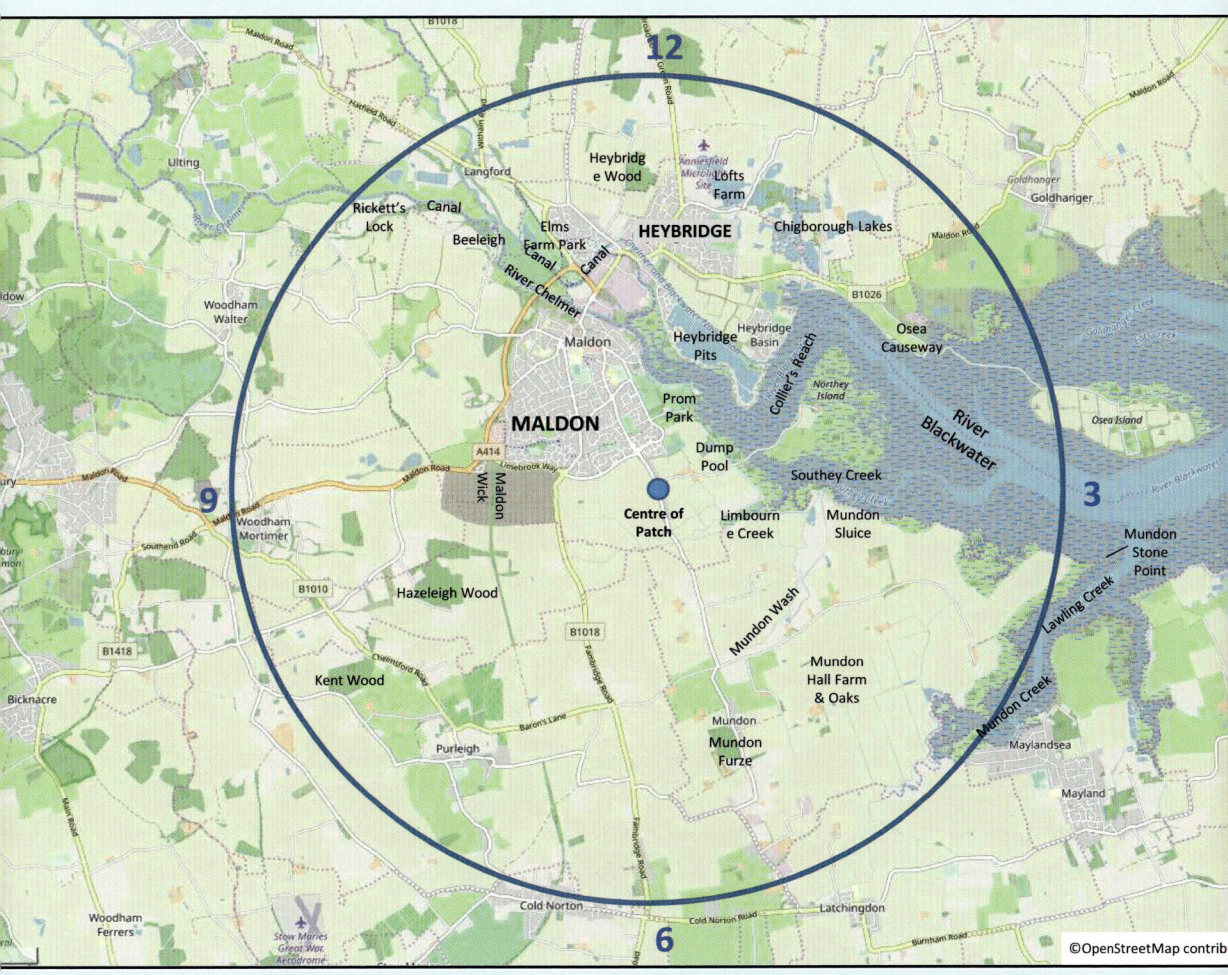

In the map, the blue circle depicts the boundary of "The Patch" — our Maldon study area.

Treating the area as a clock face, and dividing the area into four by means of the hours, then principal sites referred to in the book are located as follows:

Between 9 & 12
The majority of Maldon Town
The tidal section of the River Chelmer
Beeleigh (abbey, weir & falls)
Chelmer & Blackwater Navigation (canal)
Elms Farm Park
Heybridge Wood

Between 6 & 3
Farmland
Purleigh
Kent Wood
Hazeleigh Wood
Maldon Wick (old Railway Line)

Between 12 & 3
The Prom Park
Heybridge Pits
Lofts Farm & Chigborough Lakes
The Dump Pool (near the recycling centre)
The Blackwater River & Estuary
Southey Creek & Northey Island

Between 3 & 6
Limbourne Creek
Mundon Sluice
Mundon Wash
Mundon Hall Farm & Oaks
Mundon Furze (woodland)

Our patch stretches from Mundon and Purleigh in the south towards Great Totham in the north and from Woodham Mortimer in the west to the edges of Osea Island and Lawling Creek in the east.

This definition has served us well over the years and has been reinforced through being used as the basis of a number of our birding contests including 24 hour and year-listing challenges. There has never been a serious move to change the boundaries though it is possible that if a major rarity were to be found just outside then the border might need to be stretched!

As is the norm with other birdwatchers' local patches, we count birds seen from wherever we are within the area of our patch, whether on the ground or in the air space above it. In theory if we stood on the sea wall with a powerful enough telescope then we could include records of birds flying over Bradwell but in reality, all the species on our patch list have been seen or reliably heard within its boundaries. (Quail is the only species on the list that has not been physically seen- they are so good at staying hidden that despite much effort, none of the three individuals heard calling were actually sighted!).

A field of Meadow Buttercup alongside the canal at Langford (SW)

2
THE GEOLOGY AND EARLIER NATURAL HISTORY OF MALDON

Geology and Climate

Over the last few million years the climate has alternated between spells of warmth, indeed warmer than today, to periods of intense cold. During the coldest stage of the Anglian glaciation, 450,000 years ago, there were huge ice-caps up to 1,000 metres thick sitting as close to Maldon as Chelmsford. There would have been little life in the region then but the associated glaciers were responsible for shaping the landscape you see today, by depositing huge amounts of material and by diverting the River Thames from its route out to the north of Colchester, into its present position that we are so familiar with.

There followed a series of further freezes, culminating in the Devensian glaciation, which extended south to present day Norfolk and peaked around 27,000 years ago.

When the Ice Ages ended, some 10,000 years ago, the climate could well have been similar to that which we are experiencing now, with the flora and fauna of similar forms to those we recognise today. The countryside would have been in a virgin state, with higher ground covered in mixed, deciduous, "wildwood" and with river valleys opening into extensive floodplains, with swampy reedbeds and grassy edges, bounded by alder and sallow. Some time after the last ice age, modern man arrived in Essex, and since then he has slowly but surely been altering and changing the landscape, flora and fauna, a process that has accelerated rapidly in the last hundred years.

Maldon town itself sits atop a hill composed of boulder clay, "London Clay", whilst Heybridge rests on mostly sandy loams, created by past riparian action. Beneath these sandy loams are sands and gravels, much of which has since been extracted commercially for use in road building and the construction industry.

Natural Prehistory

The oldest fossils locally can be found upon the foreshores of Northey and Osea Islands where, within the clay, there are the remains of crinoids, a group of marine animals that still survive today but were found in far greater numbers and diversity in the past. More recent evidence of natural prehistory has been found by excavation, mostly as a consequence of the sand and gravel industry.

Most gravel pits were dug without any real watching brief from archaeologists, palaeontologists or geologists. Hence much will have been lost. However, a chance discovery in the 1980s brought to light the incredible fauna that lived and died in and around Maldon some 20,000 years ago. During the digging of Lofts Farm gravel pit, a layer of peat was revealed that contained the bones of a cold-climate mammal fauna from the last Ice Age, including Woolly Mammoth, Woolly Rhinoceros, Giant Deer, Reindeer, Bison, Spotted Hyena and Wolf. They point to a tundra-like environment being present around Maldon at the time, although modern man was not going to be strolling up the "Market Hill to be" for another 15,000 years or so.

So far, the earliest physical evidence of birds in the area has come from amongst Roman remains discovered in an archaeological dig prior to the construction of the Blackwater estate in Heybridge in the 1990s and comprised the bones of Mute Swan, ducks, Peregrine, Woodcock, Curlew, and Raven.

Early Ornithologies

Prior to the 20th century, the wildlife of Essex was little chronicled. Most records were of species shot, either for food or for display cabinets. The first major treatise was published in 1890: Miller Christy's *"The Birds of Essex, A Contribution to the Natural History of the County"*.

Its chapters on wildfowling and falconry ("hawking") may seem dated now but it does portray a county with vibrant populations of farmland birds. Mention is made of a number of species now much scarcer. Christy quotes a letter discussing Bitterns, noting that they were *"not unfrequently met with upon the marshes by the side of the river which runs* (to Maldon)". That Bitterns were previously commoner is reflected in the naming of the village of Purleigh, which was originally known as Purlea — "Bittern clearing".

Purleigh village sign (with Bittern)

Christy fully acknowledges assistance given to him in his work by E. A. Fitch, past mayor of Maldon and President of the Essex Field Club, whose own "Maldon and the River Blackwater", first published in 1894, remains a classic history of our locality. In those days there would have been more rough ground and scattered trees and hedgerows. Christy records Fitch as having found nesting Tree Pipit and Wryneck locally and a Nightjar nest at Hazeleigh. All three of these species have long since ceased breeding in our area. Another bird more regular then was the Hooded Crow — birds would arrive here from the continent each year, especially in harsh weather.

People living in previous centuries seem generally to have had a much closer awareness of the birds around them than those inhabiting modern times. This is reflected in the way that traditional local names for birds so aptly described the way they were encountered, such as "Wall Bird" (Spotted Flycatcher), "Mudlark" (Rock Pipit) and "Butcher Bird" (Red-backed Shrike).

Even then there were species in decline across Essex, with Raven, Hobby, Red-backed Shrike and Woodlark amongst those noted. However Tree Sparrow were still present in flocks and House Sparrow considered a pest.

On to 1929 and William Glegg's *A History of the Birds of Essex*. This all new work captured circumstances a century ago and his detailed research discovered a number of interesting records regarding Maldon. Both Raven and Red Kite were persecuted in the 19th century and had been wiped out by Glegg's time however he records Raven as having previously nested on Northey Island and at various farms around Mundon. He records the last Essex nest of Red Kite having been near Maldon in 1854. Common Buzzard was long gone as a breeder although it was still an irregular winter visitor (Glegg recorded two having been trapped at Hazeleigh Wood in February 1928). In the 1920s there was a heronry in a plantation by Mundon Church, at the time one of only six current heronries in Essex.

Up to the Present Day

The next relevant treatise on Essex birdlife was published in more modern times, in 1968: *A Guide to the Birds of Essex* by Robert Hudson and Geoffrey A. Pyman. This provided the latest status of the county's birds along with a summary of past and recent records. Geoffrey Pyman developed his interest in nature while studying at Maldon Grammar School and so knew Maldon well. Publication came at a time when the combined effects of direct persecution and indirect poisoning from pesticides meant raptor populations were at an all-time low — in 1966 there were only two known breeding pairs of Sparrowhawk in the whole of the county and between 1964 and 1966 only 40 breeding pairs of Kestrel were found.

Collared Dove, Maldon, Dec 2020

First appearing in the UK in the 1950, they are now a widespread and common garden bird

By the time of Hudson and Pyman's guide, Collared Doves had arrived and were 'locally numerous and increasing rapidly'. Willow Warblers were still commoner than Chiffchaff. Wintering Blackcap and Chiffchaff were now starting to be noted.

"A *New Guide to the Birds of Essex*", compiled by Dr Simon Cox and published in 1984, was a completely fresh review. It incorporated results generated by organised fieldwork, including the 1968–1972 national survey organised by the British Trust for Ornithology and the Birds of Estuaries Enquiry, sponsored by the Nature Conservancy Council. Using quantified data, the book was able to identify the national and international importance of the Blackwater Estuary for wintering wildfowl and wading birds. The book mentions the impacts of agricultural, industrial and urban developments. Red-backed Shrikes had ceased to breed but on a positive note, the beginnings of recovery of raptor fortunes and the first contemporary breeding records of Avocet were highlighted as well as the first Essex occurrences of Cetti's Warbler.

The most recent and most comprehensive review up to and into the 21st century is Simon Wood's own six hundred page tome *"The Birds of Essex"*, published in 2007. As well as current status, it includes detailed coverage of the history of birds and bird recording within the county. (Further details of this work and of other relevant publications, such as John Dobson and Darren Tansley's excellent *"Mammals of Essex"*, can be found in the reference section at the back of this book).

3
MALDON NOW

A mosaic of different habitats...

Present day Maldon comprises a wide range of habitats, dominated by farmland, housing development and, distinctly, the Blackwater and Chelmer river system, inlaid with a selection of freshwater gravel pits, woods and parkland. The following sections describe this variety which, together, explain why the biodiversity of Maldon is so rich.

The Estuary and Northey Island

For many birders the abiding memory of Maldon is the view from the sea wall across the estuary, with acres of low tide mud covered by a myriad of different birds.

While mudflats may appear to provide little in the way of nutrition, with limited vegetation beyond green algae, eelgrass and samphire, the sediment they contain

View of wintering wildfowl and waders from the sea wall (Wigeon in foreground)

Maldon Mud Run June 2018. Originally a winter event, it now takes place in the spring but still remains a significant challenge, as the lead author can confirm!

is highly productive, hosting a range of marine invertebrates including molluscs, crustaceans and worms such as lugworms and ragworms.

During winter months, thousands of wading birds depend on this cornucopia, different species evolving different strategies to catch different prey, from the deep probing Curlew and godwits to the short-billed Dunlin and Ringed Plover, pecking at or just below the surface.

Maldon mud also contains much of the detritus of human habitation laced with marine oil and other pollutants from historic shipping activities. This nevertheless does not deter the hundreds of people who wade through it during the annual Maldon charity Mud Run!

The relatively low rainfall in this part of Essex results in increased salinity of the river. It is thought that salt makers have harvested sea salt from the area for 2,000 years. There is still some evidence of early workings just east of Mundon Sluice. Nowadays most salt consumption has moved to rock salt, which is more economical to produce. Nevertheless, the Maldon Salt Company, founded in 1882, continues to take salt from the Blackwater estuary using traditional methods and to supply discerning restaurants and home cooks, both nationally and internationally.

Wildfowling was another major pursuit based around the creeks and marshes of the Blackwater. In the early 18th century, the novelist Daniel Defoe wrote of the area around Osea Island *"so well known by our London men of pleasure for the infinite number of wild fowl, that is to say, duck, mallard, teal, and wigeon, of which there are such vast flights, that they tell us the island, namely the creek, seems covered with them at certain times of the year"*. Duck decoy ponds and traps were created such as one on the eastern side of Northey Island and another at Cobb's Farm, on the Goldhanger Road. This commercial activity increased in the 19th century with the advent of the punt gun which could be over nine feet long with a bore of an inch and a half or more. In fact, one of the earliest designs of punt for carrying these guns was built by the Buckle family of Maldon.

The level of hunting tailed off during the early 20th century. However, significant areas of marsh are still owned by local wildfowling clubs who now play a stewardship role in maintaining their attractiveness for ducks and, in consequence, for other wildlife too. The number of birds now shot is low.

The topography of the estuary has changed little since the late 18th century. The sea wall generally still follows its original course, separating town and farmland from the river and protecting against big tides, though the walls were not built up to their current form until after the floods of 1953. There remain large areas of saltmarsh, acting as a buffer against tidal action and providing the walk eastwards with the timeless vistas that on grey days can readily conjure up the atmosphere Charles Dickens depicted so eloquently in Great Expectations.

The wildlife value of the Blackwater estuary as a whole was recognised by its 1995 designation as a 'Ramsar' site — a wetland of international importance, and added to the list of key sites established by UNESCO at their Convention on Wetlands at Ramsar. This listing is based on the estuary's extent and diversity of habitat, the invertebrate fauna (including British Red Data Book species), the flora and the internationally significant bird populations, particularly of Dark-bellied Brent Goose and Icelandic Black-tailed Godwit. (There is more information on these key species in Chapter 4).

↑ Marsh Samphire, abundant around the edge of the saltmarsh
↓ Saltmarsh with Sea Lavender, Southey Creek

The saltmarsh is home to specialist communities of plants that can survive the saline conditions and regularly being submerged. At lower levels, flooded by every tide, glassworts predominate (these include the Marsh Samphire well known to chefs — popular with Sea Bass!). Higher up, where conditions are less arduous, there is more variety, such as Sea Purslane and Cordgrass (an invasive species but playing a role in holding the marsh together). At the very top, along the edge of the sea wall, are species such as Sea Beet and Sea Aster that spend most of their life above the waterline but are hardy enough to survive an occasional spring tide dunking.

While most of the year the saltmarsh presents a palette of grey-greens and subtle browns, during the summer, its whole appearance transforms successively as different flowers come into bloom. First the white of Scurvy Grass, then the purple of drifts of Sea Lavender followed by the yellow-centred Sea Aster, at the top of the marsh. Finally, towards the later months, there are fiery reddish hues as the foliage of the glassworts takes on their autumnal colours.

Great views of the marsh can be had from the coastal footpath that runs out from Maldon along both north and south banks of the estuary, part of the 75 mile Saltmarsh Coast Trail that traces the boundary of Maldon District. The southerly route leads from the Prom Park past Maldon Sailing Club and the recycling centre in the direction of Maylandsea.

The saltmarsh opens up around **Northey Island** — a tidal island, linked to the mainland by a causeway which is covered for a few hours over high tide. The island is owned by the National Trust and is traditionally linked to the Battle of Maldon as it has been taken to be the site where the Vikings landed before proceeding over the causeway to do battle with the Anglo Saxons on the land which is now part of South House Farm. However, as the local topography has probably changed significantly since the Dark Ages, there are those who now think that the true site of the battle may have been over towards present day Heybridge or even at Osea.

Northey Island has some interesting old ornithological records. In 1896, E. A. Fitch found a Short-eared Owl nest there with eleven young. Fitch also reported

The causeway to Northey Island (covered at High Tide)

that for many years, Ravens used an old elm on the island as their "Raven tree" — a traditional nest site.

For a long period, Northey Island was farmed for arable crops but it was inundated during the floods of 1897, since which time saltmarsh took over. In 1991 some pioneering work was carried out to realign part of the sea wall to increase the area available to saltmarsh to mitigate against loss of this now scarce habitat due to sea level rise, the first such 'Managed Realignment' project in England. Having proved successful (and now emulated elsewhere in the country) further work has been carried out along the southern embankment of Northey during 2019 and 2020.

From the causeway, the southerly sea wall footpath carries on past **Limbourne Creek** and then to **Mundon Sluice**, at which point Osea Island comes into view, and then onwards to the edge of our patch and beyond.

The sea wall and saltmarsh stretching far into the distance eastwards from Mundon Sluice. As they say on the Maldon District Ultra Marathon — "Out on the Dengie Peninsula, no one can hear you scream!"

The sea wall along the northern bank of the river can be accessed via Daisy Meadow car park in Heybridge Basin. After walking past the pubs by the lock you pass Blackwater Sailing Club and then extensive static caravan parks and eventually reach the causeway to **Osea Island**. The island has a colourful history, from Neolithic times onwards. It is currently in private hands and recording studios have been installed. It has been used as a film set in recent years — much of the 2012 movie *The Woman in Black* was filmed there.

After the causeway, the sea wall passes a sewage works and then a long pool surrounded by reedbed while along the edge of the river there is then an area of wildfowling marsh as the sea wall begins to twist and turn towards Goldhanger.

The further you walk along the sea wall, particularly along the southern bank, the fewer other people you will encounter and the wilder the experience will become…

Heybridge Gravel Pits

At the head of the estuary lie Heybridge Pits. Created by the flooding of exhausted gravel excavations, the pits current manifestation is as a divided area of brackish lakes lying between the estuary and canal. With some small reedbeds, scrub and views over the Blackwater it is the most diverse and, on occasion, rewarding birding location on the patch. With views over to Northey Island, the Prom and the Hythe, the sea wall footpath is also extremely popular with photographers, especially in the early evening as the sun sets behind Maldon Town.

There are different avian attractions all year round, ranging from Cuckoo and warblers in the spring, the thriving Black-headed Gull colony and nesting Common Tern in the summer, through to wintering wildfowl and niche species such as Bearded Tit and Stonechat. A key feature is the use of the pits as a roosting site for Black-tailed Godwit.

Heybridge Pits with roosting Black-tailed Godwit, Sept 2015 (SW)

Breeding Avocet, Heybridge Pits, May 2011 (SP) (Common Tern in background)

Located where the estuary narrows, the Pits are often a stopping off point for birds flying up the river and then finding they have reached the end of the open water. It is a good site for passage waders though seeing them often requires an early morning visit, before the muddy fringes of the Pits have been disturbed by walkers and their canine companions.

In some years Avocet and Little Ringed Plover have bred. Unfortunately, there are currently limited nest sites for them — the islands are very vulnerable to water level changes and the edges of the pits, to disturbance. They also have to run the gauntlet with the gulls though for such elegant birds, Avocet are surprisingly feisty and can put up a spirited defence.

The brackish water provides habitat for many different creatures, including brine shrimp, and fish such as Carp, Bream and Eel. Some of the Carp have grown to a large size, no doubt hoovering up many of the smaller forms of life in the process.

There was a period during the 1970s early 1980s when water levels were much lower and the marshier conditions were a magnet for scarcer waders, with regular Ruff, Spotted Redshank and Wood Sandpiper along with a variety of rarer species such as

Long-billed Dowitcher, White-rumped and Pectoral Sandpiper, Temminck's Stint, and Red-necked Phalarope. An adult Caspian Tern spent three days at the Pits in June 1981, to the delight of visiting birdwatchers. At the end of the 1990s, the old chalet area at the western end, where Little Owl and Stonechat nested, was cleared and building work commenced for a new housing estate.

The status of the Pits has been somewhat confused in recent years. When the new housing developments at the end of Hall Road were approved, it was anticipated that the pits would be managed for wildlife. However in reality, apart from the erection of some poorly constructed birdwatching hides and a number of information boards, very little was done. The one real positive was the creation of some small islands which have since been used by nesting birds including Common Tern and increasing numbers of Black-headed Gulll.

In 2016 and 2018, applications were made by a potential purchaser of the site to establish commercial fishing. These specific proposals were refused by Maldon District Council due to concerns over the wildlife interest as well as over access issues.

In 2019 an appeal to the Planning Inspectorate was dismissed, citing potentially damaging collateral impacts to the ecology of the estuary itself as one of the main issues.

Increased observations by Simon Wood, following a move to Heybridge, have led to a host of new discoveries, from orchids to mining bees. It is to be hoped in the future that a more permanent protective state can be secured and that proper habitat management can be carried out. There is no doubt that there is great potential to improve the site for wildlife, for example by actively controlling water levels and quality and through the construction of more islands to allow more birds to nest and roost in peace.

Pyramidal Orchid, Heybridge Pits, June 2021 (SW)

Beeleigh Weir and Falls, a good spot to look for the regular breeding pair of Grey Wagtail

River and Canal

Upstream from Heybridge Pits, the tidal reach of the main river continues under Fullbridge, past the Sunny Sailor and the Tesco supermarket, under the bypass, past the golf course and all the way to **Beeleigh**. Here, the river is fed by the canal — there are two weirs to allow overflow from the upstream navigation into the river while the main course of the canal heads via lock gates towards Heybridge. The area's bridges and pathways, along with multiple watercourses and engineering works, produce a variety of perspectives and views that make it a wonderful place for a contemplative stroll and a magnet for photographers. Through the good will of the landowner, it has been possible to park just before the bridge over to the golf course and there are popular walks from here both along the towpath as well as over the old metal footbridge towards Beeleigh Mill and Beeleigh Abbey.

The narrow bridge skirting the main weir provides a great vantage point for watching the Mallard and Mute Swan that frequent the area in the regularly fulfilled hope of people feeding them. At lower states of tide, the mud and shingle are worth checking for foraging Grey Wagtail and Common Sandpiper. At any point a Kingfisher may fly by. Fish to be found on the tidal river include Mullet and Dab. Both Sea Bass and Eel have been watched scaling the weir to reach the fresh water of the canal. During the 19th century several large Sturgeon were caught in the area, including a 131lb specimen near Beeleigh Mill.

Beeleigh Mill originally had two water wheels that between them powered ten grinding stones, used to produce flour that was shipped by barge to bakeries in London. There was also a later steam engine, powering additional stones, that is currently being restored.

Here too, on the south side of the river, lies **Beeleigh Abbey**. The abbey was established in 1180 by the 'White Canons' a Catholic order founded in Prémontré in north-eastern France. It has had a varied history, including damage sustained during the dissolution of the monasteries during Tudor times. A succession of owners in the 20th century restored the building. The latest actions gained an award from the Royal Institution of Chartered Surveyors. The Abbey and its grounds have a timeless character, with Peacock strutting across the lawns and ornamental Fantail Pigeon keeping watch from the roofs of the outbuildings. In recent years these grounds have been made available to the public during periodic open days during the summer.

Upstream of Beeleigh, the freshwater Chelmer and Blackwater Navigation leads up towards the city of Chelmsford. Nowadays there is little traffic. There is no connection to other navigable waterways and so only a few barges and canoeists and, more recently, paddle boarders make use of it. Generally, the feel is that of a peaceful backwater.

Beeleigh Abbey, July 2010

Ricketts Lock, the next lock upstream from Beeleigh and at the limit of our patch

The canal itself is full of wildlife, a testament to the recently much improved quality of the water. Anglers can fish for Roach, Bream, Tench, Chub, Perch, Pike, Dace, Barbel and Carp. In the summer, Banded Demoiselle and other damselflies swarm around the banks while their larger cousins, including chasers and Emperor Dragonfly, patrol midstream.

The navigation is lined by a variety of trees. Around Beeleigh there are Alder, attractive to parties of Siskin in the winter. Further upstream are poplars and different willows, including some commercially planted for cricket bat production — 'Cricket Bat Willow'. The tow path passes pasture, full of buttercups in the summer, and some majestic old trees, favoured by Kestrels and Tawny Owls.

Keep on walking and you reach Ricketts Lock, marking the western border of our patch. If you are enjoying yourself you could of course carry on, past Hoe Mill, Ulting Church and eight further sets of locks to Springfield and then Chelmsford, almost 14 miles from Heybridge Basin. Be warned if you require refreshment: there are, perhaps surprisingly, no pubs along the towpath — so make the most of the tea and cakes available at Papermill Lock!

More Gravel Pits and Inland Waters

Other expanses of fresh water can be found in the complex of flooded gravel pits and lakes to the north-east of Heybridge. The majority are fished — some for Carp and other coarse fish, while others are stocked with trout for fly fishermen. Of these, the key wildlife sites are the pits at Lofts Farm and Chigborough Lakes.

Lofts Farm Pits

To the north of Scraley Road there are two flooded pits at Lofts Farm. Breeding birds include Great Crested Grebe, Greylag, Canada and Egyptian Geese and, if water levels permit, Black-headed Gull. For a few years a Black-necked Grebe summered, occasionally accompanied by a second bird. However breeding was never proven and since fishing activity increased there have been no further records. During winter, flocks of diving ducks and Coot gather.

The waters nurture a great number of insects which in turn attract aerial feeding birds that can catch them on the wing, such as hirundines (swallows and martins) as well as Common Tern and occasional Black Tern and Little Gull.

Little Gull, Lofts Farm Pits, April 2019 (SP)

It has been the best local site for Hobby when on balmy evenings, these acrobatic falcons may, with luck, be spotted in hot pursuit of hirundines and dragonflies.

Looking north from the footpath between the lakes there are views of distant fields, the haunts of Brown Hare, Skylark and assorted geese, and far off Common Buzzard can often be spotted, soaring on thermals rising above South Wood. This same spot can also offer a good opportunity in the evening for spying Barn Owl hunting noiselessly along the hedgerows.

Chigborough Lakes Essex Wildlife Trust Reserve

Chigborough Lakes Nature Reserve sits between Scraley and Chigborough Roads. Its 46 acres are managed by Essex Wildlife Trust and contain a variety of habitats, including open water, small ponds, waterlogged wooded terrain (willow carr) and Blackthorn/ Hawthorn scrub. The reduced disturbance through lack of fishing means that there is an increased number and variety of nesting bird species compared with neighbouring sites.

Common Spotted Orchid, Chigborough Lakes, June 2013 (JB)

Amongst the plants here are Pedunculate and Sessile Oak, Ash and eleven or more different types of willow including numerous hybrids. Interesting wild flowers include colonies of Common Spotted Orchid and Broad-leaved Helleborine.

The key ornithological feature is the presence of our area's only current heronry. In the previous century there was a heronry at Mundon Hall, last used in 1974, and one on Osea Island, from where birds moved over to Osea Road where they nested for the first few years of our study period. Grey Heron began nesting at Chigborough Lakes in 1992, when 5 pairs bred. This number has gradually increased: thirteen nesting pairs were counted during the 2018 national survey of heronries. The reserve's suitability as a secure site for large, tree-nesting birds to raise their chicks has since been aptly demonstrated by the arrival of colonising Egret and Cormorant as well.

Little Egret are a newcomer as a breeding bird in the UK, with the first pairs nesting this side of the English Channel in 1996. They only began breeding in Essex in 2000 so it was with some excitement that pairs were found within the heronry at Chigborough Lakes in summer 2002 with successful nesting beginning the year after. The site is now home to an established colony: ten nests were counted in the 2018 survey. Larger numbers of egrets come from further afield to use Chigborough Lakes as a roost site — at some times of the year over a hundred individuals have been logged arriving at dusk.

Traditionally the British race of Cormorant (*carbo*) has been a coastal nesting species and was generally only a winter visitor to Maldon. During the seventies, a steady increase in the appearance of the tree-nesting Continental race (*sinensis*) in South East England most likely prompted the start of inland breeding at Abberton Reservoir in 1981. This habit of inland breeding has now spread throughout South East England, the Midlands and beyond with both races now nesting together, the tree-nesting proclivity having been adopted by *carbo* birds as well. They first began breeding around our area in 2010 when they started nesting in the trees on the main fishing lake island at Lofts Farm. After a few years however, disturbance from fishing activities became too much for them and they moved across Scraley Road to join the herons at Chigborough Lakes.

The first family of Cattle Egret to be raised in Essex, Chigborough Lakes, June 2019 (JB)

Hot news in June 2019, during the writing of this book, was the discovery by the authors of Essex's first breeding Cattle Egret within the Chigborough heronry. They defended their nest site against all intruders and successfully raised four chicks.

The lakes within the reserve also hold breeding Great Crested and Little Grebe as well as Mute Swan and various ducks, while the woody margins have healthy populations of Bullfinch, Treecreeper and both Green and Great Spotted Woodpecker as well as Muntjac Deer. Tawny Owl nest in the older trees.

In winter there are good numbers of dabbling ducks, in particular Gadwall and Shoveler, and a smaller increase in diving ducks: Tufted Duck and Common Pochard. Alder and Silver and Downy Birch attract winter finches, such as Siskin and Lesser Redpoll, while Water Rail can be heard skulking in the reeds.

The main winter spectacle however has been the increasing use of the bushes and trees at the back of the main lake as a night time roost by hundreds of corvids-mainly Jackdaw though with good numbers of Rook and Carrion Crow as well. As they prepare to leave the site around dawn and then take off in swirling clouds, the noise can be almost deafening!

The other main set of lakes in the area is managed by Chigborough Farm, including Chigboro' Fisheries, catering for both trout and coarse anglers and including a match lake complex. There is a fishing lodge and nearby restaurant, smokehouse and delicatessan. The principal lake, Home Water, is large and open and generally holds a good selection of ducks, with Little Egret often to be found around the edges and geese, including Egyptian, on the well-cut grassy banks.

To the west and south of Maldon, a couple of other fishing lakes are of note: Ricketts Mere, adjacent to the canal, and the newly created fishing lake north of the A414 by Limebrook Farm. The latter can be viewed from the footpath that runs up the hill opposite the stables and looks perfect for a passing Osprey!

Farmland

The majority of land around Maldon is farmed, as has been the case for hundreds and possibly thousands of years. Whilst Limebrook Way was being constructed,

Cattle by the borrow dyke at South House Farm, Nov 2010

to the south of Maldon, evidence was found of a Roman farmstead and it has been thought that some of the field alignments in this area date back to Roman times.

The 1086 Domesday Book makes mention of Maldon and surrounding homesteads and lists numbers of sheep, pigs and cows and plough teams within the district. In the past the fields must have been very colourful with flowers such as Cornflower, Common Poppy and Corn Marigold in amongst the wheat and barley. Indeed nearby Goldhanger was named for the profusion of marigolds seen there in summer.

Nowadays the focus locally is mainly on arable farming, with wheat, oilseed rape and hay being the principal crops. Besides these staples, others such as barley and lucerne have also been grown in recent years, depending on customer demand, economics and the need for rotation to maintain nutrients within the soil. The growing cycle provides a changing habitat for a range of typical farmland birds, from breeding Skylark and Corn Bunting through Black-headed Gull following the plough to wintering Golden Plover.

Lucerne at harvest time, Aug 2013

There are still some cattle raised, such as the regular small herds of young steers kept on the National Trust land at South House Farm and grazed during the summer in fields along the sea wall and beside Limbourne Creek. These cattle often have attendant parties of Starling, attracted by the insects they disturb. In late summer, Yellow Wagtail join them too, sometimes in quite large numbers (over a hundred were there together in August 2020!). The area around Limbourne Creek is a last remnant of the traditional grazing marshes that have essentially long gone from the Maldon area.

Fields are also managed as pasture for horses — there are a number of stables throughout the area, along with associated paddocks. These stables are haunts of Pied Wagtail and Swallow while the paddocks attract a range of species including thrushes and gulls during the winter.

Farmers face ongoing challenges as they try to maximise food production whilst keeping costs down and so competition from hungry wildlife must be a concern.

The most damaging avian 'pests' are the large winter flocks of Woodpigeon that can carpet fields and are particularly drawn to autumn-sown oilseed rape. In coastal fields, Brent Geese cause damage not just through their foraging but also by trampling emergent vegetation under their webbed feet.

Over the last century, farming methods have become increasingly intensive, with more crop cycles per year and industrial scale use of fertilisers, insecticides and herbicides. The resulting sterilisation and homogenisation of the habitat has greatly impacted our bird populations, with fewer Yellowhammer, Skylark and partridge and the lack of flying insects has no doubt thwarted feeding Swallow and House Martin. On the other hand, some local landowners and farmers at least are taking positive action to create wildlife-friendly habitat. This topic is discussed in more detail later in Chapter 12.

Hedgerows and Edgelands

As elsewhere, fields around Maldon have been traditionally bounded by hedgerows, providing both food and shelter for wildlife. The most prevalent species are Hawthorn and Blackthorn — with blossom in spring and haws and sloes in the autumn, the

Field boundary south of Limebrook Way

latter an annual attraction for the district's gin drinkers! Typically, older hedgerows contain a wider variety of plants and trees. Bigger trees, particularly, play an important role in providing song posts for thrushes and occasional Cuckoo as well as giving Carrion Crow somewhere to nest and, where there are suitable holes, Little Owl.

The vegetation at the foot of hedges is perfect habitat for rodents- food for Kestrel and Barn Owl and, anywhere near housing, pet cats too. As is well known, despite being fed at home, many cats still choose to spend the night following their instincts in hunting anything they are quick enough to catch.

Hedgerows also provide a valuable role in linking other patches of habitat such as woods, acting as conduits for any bats that are averse to crossing open country.

Sadly, around Maldon as in much of the rest of the country, many miles of hedges have been stripped out to create larger fields or to be replaced by fences which are more easily maintained. Those that do remain are often severely damaged each year through inappropriate 'pruning' with mechanised cutters that indiscriminately level anything in their path. Nevertheless, there are good hedgerows remaining, often away from roads in locations such as along the sea wall, where mechanical pruning is more problematic. These provide homes to Yellowhammer, Linnet and Common Whitethroat and Lesser Whitethroat amongst others and are also popular with passing migrants in spring and autumn. We are fortunate that we still have sufficient bushes and fence posts at field boundaries where Corn Bunting can perch and sing out their jangling springtime refrains.

Maldon Wick Essex Wildlife Trust Reserve

An unintended consequence of the closure of the railways into and out of Maldon has been the development of some areas of quality wildlife habitat where the trains used to run. The best example is what is left of the embankment of the Maldon to Woodham Ferrers line to the south of the town. A length of a mile and a half at Maldon Wick (just south of Morrisons Supermarket), along with an adjoining meadow, was bequeathed to the Essex Wildlife Trust by Peter Mann in 1986 and is now managed as a nature reserve.

Trees and shrubs have grown up along its length, including both Wild Service and Spindle, and it has proved popular for wild flowers, warblers and butterflies (a speciality is White-letter Hairstreak). The larger trees provide a haunt for Tawny Owl and there are Badger too. In 1998 a pond was constructed as mitigation for the loss of a pond during car park construction for the nearby supermarket. This has developed into an excellent site for dragonflies and damselflies. Water lilies, with their expansive leaves, provide attractive landing pads for many of the damselflies.

Maldon Wick
Essex Wildlife
Trust Reserve,
July 2009

Various fish have been 'liberated' into the pond, including Goldfish, which are no doubt part of the attraction to visiting Grey Heron and Kingfisher. Moorhen breed. Other wildlife interest includes woodpeckers, Jay and occasional Nightingale.

Despite it being part of the nature reserve, the pond has unfortunately had a lot of disturbance from dogs encouraged to go for a swim. A further, recently recognised, concern is that if dogs have had their fur treated for fleas, the chemical insecticides can wash off into water where they swim and harm the invertebrates whose home it is.

Woodland

To the west and north our patch starts edging on to some fairly extensive areas of interlinked woodland on the higher ground around Woodham Walter/ Danbury and towards Great Totham and Wickham Bishops. However, our main focus has been closer to the centre of the patch, where there are a handful of isolated significant woods, along with some smaller areas of established trees dotted around the parks and gravel pits and along the canal. It is these more local sites that are considered in the paragraphs to follow.

Hazeleigh Hall Wood (hereafter referred to as Hazeleigh Wood) lies to the south of the town towards Woodham Mortimer. It is ancient woodland, mentioned in the Domesday Book as a foraging site for pigs. Mainly deciduous, the dominant trees are Hornbeam, Oaks (Turkey as well as Pedunculate and Sessile), Hazel and Ash. The age of the woodland is reflected in the presence of less common native trees, including Midland Hawthorn, Wild Service Tree and Field Maple, as well as flowers such as Dog's Mercury and Yellow Archangel. It was clear-felled for timber during the

English Bluebell, Hazeleigh Wood, Apr 2011. Careful management has led to a superb annual display.

Second World War but fortunately the land wasn't turned over to any alternative use and so the seed bed survived relatively intact. The woodland became re-established although, with minimal direct management, it became overgrown and too dense to allow much light through to encourage those plants trying to survive at ground level.

Since 1993 the major part of the wood has been owned and managed by John and Maureen Bissell. Through their energy and sheer hard work the wood has been opened up and revived and it is now a home to a great diversity of fauna and flora. Careful coppicing has encouraged Nightingale — in some years double figures of these wonderful songsters have been heard, making the wood one of the premier sites in Essex for this declining species.

Throughout our study period, Hazeleigh Wood has been the most regular local site for Lesser Spotted Woodpecker, though records have recently been intermittent and it is feared it may soon be lost as a resident in the area. However Coal Tit have moved in and there have been recent Nuthatch sightings too. There is now a thriving population of White Admiral butterflies and, after a first sighting in 2018, a colony of Silver-washed Fritillary is now established, no doubt attracted by the plentiful violets within the wood, the principal food plant of their caterpillars.

↑ Lesser Spotted Woodpecker, Hazeleigh Wood, March 2017 (SW)
↗ White Admiral, Hazeleigh Wood, July 2019 (SW)

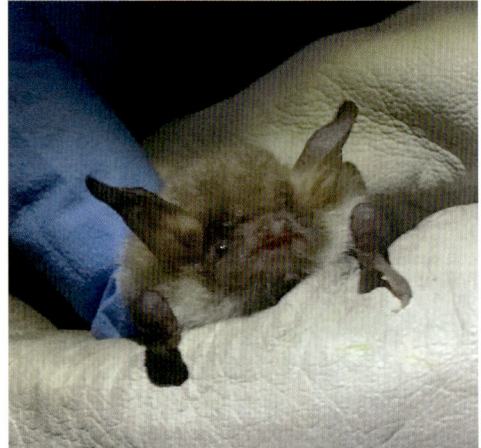

↑ Small Black Arches, Hazeleigh Wood, June 2018 (SW)
↗ Natterer's Bat, Hazeleigh Wood, Aug 2019 (JB)

Regular trapping by Simon Wood and Maureen has revealed a tremendous variety of moths at Hazeleigh Wood — so far over 670 species, including a number of regional rarities such as Small Black Arches and Dark Crimson Underwing. The Small Black Arches were the first to be seen in Essex since 1934. The wood is also good for bats — all of Essex's regular species have been recorded within the wood.

To the south west of Hazeleigh lies the smaller **Kent Wood**. Many species are similar and there is public access, with a footpath running through the middle. Breeding species here include Common Buzzard, Nuthatch, Treecreeper and Coal Tit.

At Mundon, there is another small area of ancient woodland, **Mundon Furze**, behind the village hall. It is managed by the parish council, who have decreed it to be "open for the peaceful enjoyment of all". The main trees are Oak and Ash. There are breeding Common Buzzard here too and other interest includes owls and Early Purple Orchid. Nuthatch and Firecrest have both also been recently recorded.

On the opposite side of the patch sits **Heybridge Wood**, which holds the biggest area of conifers in the area. The southern half is mainly pine, planted commercially, while the northern piece is historic deciduous woodland, with some tall firs and Holly. Unsurprisingly, this wood holds the highest local populations of the evergreen loving Coal Tit and Goldcrest. Hopefully the new housing developments in adjacent farmland will not result in excessive disturbance.

Other areas where there are sufficient concentrations of trees to attract woodland species include Chigborough, around Beeleigh, Elms Farm Park and Wood Corner Grove. Typical species occurring include Great Spotted Woodpecker, Treecreeper, Blackcap, Chiffchaff and Speckled Wood butterfly.

While there are a few old standard trees remaining along field boundaries and surviving in the fields by Hazeleigh Wood, the most striking trees in the district

The 'Petrified' Oaks at Mundon

are the 'Mundon Oaks', a gathering of 'petrified' trees close to St Mary's Church by Mundon. Standing starkly against the sky, their sun-bleached branches can take on a sinister air as they appear to grasp up to the heavens. The cause of their demise is not known for certain but may be due to a change in the water-table or salinity. It is likely their desiccation saved them from being used for war-time ship-building. Their current form, with multiple cavities and perches, makes them highly attractive to nesting Jackdaw, Stock Dove and both Little and Barn Owl.

Parks

There are two major parks in the Maldon area: the Promenade Park and Elms Farm Park.

The **Promenade Park** was opened in 1895 and became very popular with Edwardian visitors to Maldon. Set against the River Blackwater it offers great views, particularly of the Thames barges as they head in and out of the quay. It remains extremely busy to this day, though it is well looked after and on quieter days can still be a good location for birding.

The Prom Park is predominantly laid to grass, with sports pitches and general recreational areas. There are a number of standard trees of different kinds, with

The Delph Ditch in the Prom Park, Aug 2007

Horse Chestnut the most prominent. For many years there was a rookery in the trees at the western end but the Rook have now moved elsewhere. The Delph Ditch, a watercourse running across the eastern side of the park, is maintained as a wildlife area though it suffers from considerable disturbance. It is a good place for butterflies and dragonflies and over the years we have seen Water Vole, Weasel and Stoat as well as Water Rail here.

In 1905 the central Marine Lake was created, for boating and bathing. A century later it was re-configured as an ornamental lake. This change disappointed many of the local townspeople, who have memories of swimming there in their childhood, but it has proved popular for the birds, with regular breeding Mute Swan as well as Mallard, Tufted Duck, Coot, Moorhen, and Little Grebe. Other ducks such as

Gadwall and Common Pochard may sometimes be seen and in the last couple of years, Egyptian Geese have started turning up — potential future regulars.

'Limpy' the Mediterranean Gull, Prom Park, Dec 2005 (Cindy Lawes)

Reeds have been planted at either end of the lake and as they have become established, they have begun to attract Reed Warbler and, more recently, occasional Cetti's Warbler too.

For many years, the Prom Park was a haunt of 'Limpy', a Mediterranean Gull readily recognisable by his broken leg. Despite his handicap, he lived to the grand old age for a gull of at least 19 years, having first been seen (as an adult) in 1991 and last spotted in 2008. Clearly the chips that supplemented his regular diet must have been good for him!

Elms Farm Park is sited north-west of Maldon, bounded by the canal, the A414 and Heybridge Approach. Created in the 1990s, it comprises large areas of cut grass, copses and a sizeable lake. Without a car park, it is much quieter than the Prom Park though it is popular with dog walkers and joggers from nearby estates.

The canal here is great for dragonflies. It was the site where Scarce Chaser were first discovered locally and is good also for more ubiquitous species such as Four-spotted Chaser and Black-tailed Skimmer.

Lake at Elms Farm Park

Jay and Bullfinch are resident while in summer it has been a regular breeding site for Garden Warbler. Occasionally a singing Nightingale has held a territory.

On the other side of the canal there is a further expanse of greenery — Maldon Golf Course. It is relatively compact so the areas of rough grassland surrounding the well-maintained fairways are quite limited (though golfers who land their balls in this rough may not agree!). There are some stands of small trees and birds seen include Mistle Thrush and Jay. The footpath along the southern edge leads from Beeleigh to the Tesco supermarket and provides a good view of the river.

Gardens

The great majority of houses in the area have gardens, creating a patchwork habitat for wildlife as well as humans. It is true to say that the skill and enthusiasm of Maldon's gardeners varies somewhat. Some front pieces are no more than parking lots while others are a kaleidoscope of floral diversity, with plants from all corners of the world. The most common aspiration remains to have a back garden with a grass lawn surrounded by beds of flowers and shrubs intended to provide blooms for as much of the year as possible. Different fashions have led to specific themes. The increasing popularity of barbecues and outdoor eating has encouraged the installation of decking. Garden ponds are less common now, perhaps through safety fears where toddlers may be about. Those that remain may tempt Grey Heron in search of easy pickings of frogs and goldfish.

Sadly, liberal use of insecticides and weed killers has meant that populations of natural garden dwellers have been much reduced. Hedgehog have become noticeably scarcer during our study period, in part due to a reduction in slugs, one of their main natural foods. They have also been affected by a preponderance of close-fitting gates and boundary fencing, preventing them from roaming from garden to garden on their night time perambulations.

The roofs of our houses have long provided nesting sites for birds. House Sparrow and Starling capitalise on any gaps in the guttering or tiles to nest within the loft space, while House Martin site their fabrications of mud and spittle under the eaves. Bats may also make their homes in roof spaces so long as they can gain access. Traditional roof construction has often included vents in the soffits and access has been increased as roof timbers have rotted and tiles slipped. The modern fashion for tidiness and control has led to replacement of wood by maintenance-free plastic and gaps have been stopped with foam insulation, reducing the opportunities for birds. It is to be hoped that people start installing more of the now available custom designed bird (and bat) boxes to help them out.

Maldon Hall Allotments, one of three council-run allotment sites within Maldon (Cindy Lawes) Visited by a Black Redstart in December 2020

Fortunately, there are still plenty of healthy gangs of House Sparrow around Maldon and they hopefully will keep going as the tide turns, and, with greater environmental awareness, more wildlife friendly gardening methods begin to spread. The sparrows like to hang out around traditional gathering sites, making quite a racket with their chirpy gossip from within a favoured shrubby tree.

For keener vegetable gardeners there are allotments available to rent at three Maldon Town Council run sites. These can be good places to look out for the town's urban foxes though no doubt many of the gardeners themselves are not overly keen on their antics!

There are also a few larger, more formal gardens, with that at Beeleigh Abbey perhaps the most extensive. Churchyards can also offer a sanctuary for wildlife. Old Yew trees attract tits and Goldcrest and Holly berries are sought out by thrushes in the wintertime. The largest local graveyard is the Maldon Cemetery off London Road, which has a lawn section for full burials, as well as a large woodland burial site. For a short spell in 2009 the trees by the cemetery were the temporary home for an American Red-tailed Hawk — no doubt an escape from someone's aviary.

The Town

Maldon's town centre sits on a hill, indeed Maldon's name itself stems from a conjunction of the Anglo Saxon 'mael', monument, and 'dun', hill. At the highest point stands All Saints Church, with its unique 13th century triangular tower. Market Hill runs north down to Fullbridge, the principal crossing of the river, while the High Street runs south-east, branching down towards the Hythe and St Mary's, 'The Fisherman's Church', with its conspicuous white tower that has long acted as a beacon for sailors.

Old walls in the town can provide good plant habitat for species such as Rue-leaved Saxifrage and, as in this photo, Ivy-leaved Toadflax, here on the wall of the Friary Garden, June 2021 (JB)

The Rookery at Morrisons Supermarket, Mar 2020 (JB)

Typical birds to be seen around the centre include Feral Pigeon, Starling and, in more open areas, Pied Wagtail. There are enough small gardens for Robin, tits and Blackbird. The playing fields of the Plume School attract gulls, some of which have begun to bother the school's pupils as they try and snatch a share of the leftovers from packed lunches!

It can be well worth looking upwards when on the High Street to check out what might be flying over. In the summer, parties of Swift scream as they twist and turn around the rooftops. On lucky occasions, a raptor might be sighted, taking advantage of thermals rising above the town. Peregrine, Red Kite, Osprey and Honey Buzzard have all been spotted cruising overhead.

There are still a few stands of tall trees dotted about the town. As a throwback to more rural times, several have been the sites of rookeries, though there is now only

↑ Lesser Black-backed and Herring Gull nesting on industrial roof, Heybridge, June 2020 (JB)

← Male Black Redstart, Chandlers Quay, July 2020 (JB)

one still thriving, alongside the carpark at Morrisons Supermarket. In contrast another corvid, the Jackdaw, is moving in. Whilst in the early 2000s, only occasional Jackdaw were seen around the town, they are rapidly becoming more established in the way that they have already colonised nearby Danbury.

The industrial areas around The Causeway and Heybridge shopping developments may look unattractive but beauty is in the eye of the beholder, and they are the long-chosen haunt for our biggest local gang of Feral Pigeon. More recently both Herring and Lesser Black-backed Gull have started breeding here too. Following a trend for inland breeding seen elsewhere in the country, these 'seagulls' have chosen to nest on the flat roofs of industrial buildings between the canal and the river in Heybridge. To them these roofs presumably resemble the flat plateaux above island cliffs where they traditionally breed. The loose colony is a mix of the two species though currently Lesser Black-back predominate. Oystercatcher have also been seen trying to nest on these same roofs though it would seem a dangerous ploy to nest in such close proximity to these obvious predators.

Within the UK, Black Redstart is another species that likes to nest in urban and industrial settings. It is however rare, with a maximum of 80 pairs recorded as breeding nationally in 2018. So while there had been occasional previous records of birds singing in spring around Hall Road in Heybridge, it was still a pleasant surprise when Tony Kennelly found a male establishing a territory in May 2020 in the vicinity of Carr's flour mill and Chandler's Quay. Even better was to then see that it had found a mate and, a few weeks later, to see a fledgling being fed — the first proven breeding record for Maldon.

The Dump

Maldon's main refuse collection centre may seem an odd inclusion as a birdwatching site but its location by the last patch of mud to be flooded at high tide makes it a great place to watch waders at close range as they congregate before heading off to roost. Over recent years, around 30 species of waders have been seen. It has been a regular site for finding Curlew Sandpiper; rarer birds seen from here have included Grey Phalarope and both Terek and Marsh Sandpiper.

The dump is currently operating as a recycling centre, comprising about ten or so large skips for different kinds of waste material which, when full, are taken away for processing elsewhere.

In the past the dump was a traditional open tip for Maldon's trash, including all manner of food waste, and was a great attraction to hungry gulls and crows (including a Hooded Crow in May 1979). Great Black-backed Gull reached a peak winter count of 350 in January 1977, which must have been quite a sight. Numbers of these, the largest of our gulls, have rarely reached double figures since the turn of the century. The increased recycling is good for the conservation of our planet's resources but is disappointing for gull-watchers!

The open tip was filled in in the early 1990s and a balancing pool created further along the sea wall to help avoid flooding. This pool, known to local birdwatchers as the **Dump Pool**, is always worth checking for wildlife. It is subject to disturbance from walkers along the sea wall but nevertheless there is usually something to

"The Dump Pool", Sept 2009

be seen. It is shallow enough for long-legged wading birds such as Little Egret and Black-tailed Godwit to be able to feed and it has proved very attractive to wintering dabbling ducks, with sometimes a hundred or more Common Teal present. If water levels are low enough then there can be areas of exposed mud around the edges: good for occasional Common and Green Sandpiper. A variety of warblers breed around the pool including Cetti's and Reed. In some years Turtle Dove have been heard purring from the trees at the back.

Over the years, regular watching has provided some great sightings: Water Rail and Water Vole along the main ditch, Barn Owl hunting over the reeds and, during migration times, passage birds such as Garganey and Spotted Redshank.

A final spot to look at in this area is **Millennium Wood**, planted by Maldon Council on a patch of uneven ground between the dump and the leisure centre car park to celebrate the year 2000. As the trees have become established it has provided a welcome extra area of habitat. Blackcap, various tits and finches as well as Great Spotted Woodpecker can be seen and it is a regular stopover spot for migrating Chiffchaff and other warblers.

4
AN INTRODUCTION
TO THE MAIN PLAYERS

Highlights

In the opening decades of the 21st century, what are the wildlife highlights of the Maldon area?

What people enjoy is subjective but twelve experiences that we particularly look forward to are:

- Wintering Brent Geese and other wildfowl
- Waders on the mud, the flock of Golden Plover, wintering Avocet
- Winter raptors — Peregrine, Short-eared Owl and the chance of Hen Harrier and Merlin
- Sea duck and divers on the river
- Spring build-up of Black-tailed Godwit
- The first summer migrants and hearing our first Cuckoo
- Singing Nightingale and (for now at least) purring Turtle Dove
- The dawn chorus
- The mixed heronry at Chigborough
- Summer butterflies, dragonflies and moths
- The marvel of autumn migration with the chance of rarities
- Autumnal leaves and fungi

From an international perspective, the area's most significant natural role is as a wintering location for migrant waders and wildfowl (leading to the Blackwater Estuary's aforementioned listing as a Ramsar site). At the end of the 1990s, the estuary as a whole was holding average peaks of 105,000 overwintering water birds, including 4% of the world's population of Dark-bellied Brent Geese and 6.2% of the population of Icelandic Black-tailed Godwit, as well as internationally important numbers of Dunlin and Grey Plover.

Icelandic Black-tailed Godwit, Heybridge Pits, Aug 2018 (JB)
This individual was colour-ringed as an adult in northern Iceland in 2010 and sighted many times in subsequent years, at Heybridge in the autumn, Bowling Green Marsh in Devon during the winter and again in Iceland during the summer.

There are a number of different breeding populations of Brent Geese around the Arctic, sharing the scenery with Snowy Owl and Arctic Fox. Different races of Brent can be distinguished by the plumage of their flanks and bellies. The flocks that winter along the Blackwater are Dark-bellied Brent, with the scientific name *bernicla*, that have travelled amongst the furthest distances of any of our winter visitors. Their movements have been tracked as a number have had large 'Darvic' plastic rings placed on their legs with unique codes that can be read by telescope. Birds around Maldon have included some that were ringed on islands adjacent to the Taimyr Peninsula in northern Siberia and it is thought most of 'our' birds come from that general region.

In a similar way there are different populations of Black-tailed Godwit around the world. Of those that come to Maldon, the great majority are of the *islandica* race that breeds in Iceland. While some stay the winter on the estuary, others use Maldon as a staging point en route to and from wintering sites further to the south and west. As with the Brent Geese, their travels have been demonstrated through the observation of marked individuals. In the case of the godwit, plastic colour rings, in different combinations, have been put on the legs of birds while in their Icelandic breeding grounds and then looked for when they head off on migration.

A Meeting Place for Global Travellers

The enjoyment of watching birds around Maldon is greatly enhanced by how the cast of characters regularly changes through the year as migrants arrive and depart from and to all points of the compass.

In spring, a wide variety of species from Africa and the Mediterranean fly north to us in search of increased hours of daylight to feed and to raise their families. Cuckoo fitted with satellite tags have been tracked flying between East Anglia and Equatorial Africa, while Swallow ringed in Essex have been proven to travel even further, with recoveries from as far as South Africa.

We are also a sought after destination for birds to come for the winter. For somewhere so far north, our maritime climate, washed by the Gulf Stream, makes the British Isles relatively warm, hence the attraction as a wintering locale for birds looking to escape the cold continental climate of North East Europe and Western Russia.

Looking at a standard atlas projection it might seem strange that birds would also cross the North Atlantic to arrive here from Greenland and Northeast Canada but inspection of a globe shows shorter great circle routes, with some species, such as Knot, stopping over in Iceland on route. And for birds continuing south, the UK is at a pivotal point on the East Atlantic Flyway, the route taken by millions of migrants that follow the coast as they head down to Africa to winter.

In Maldon we are lucky enough to be visited by some of the planet's ultimate travellers, including Bar-tailed Godwit, Greenland Wheatear and, on occasion, passing Arctic Tern. A close relative of our locally breeding Common Tern, Arctic Tern breed in latitudes far to the north and then head south to winter around the southern oceans. Taking advantage of summer in both hemispheres, these terns probably see more daylight than any other animal species.

Arctic Tern, Heybridge Pits, Apr 2018 (SW)
One of nature's true globetrotters

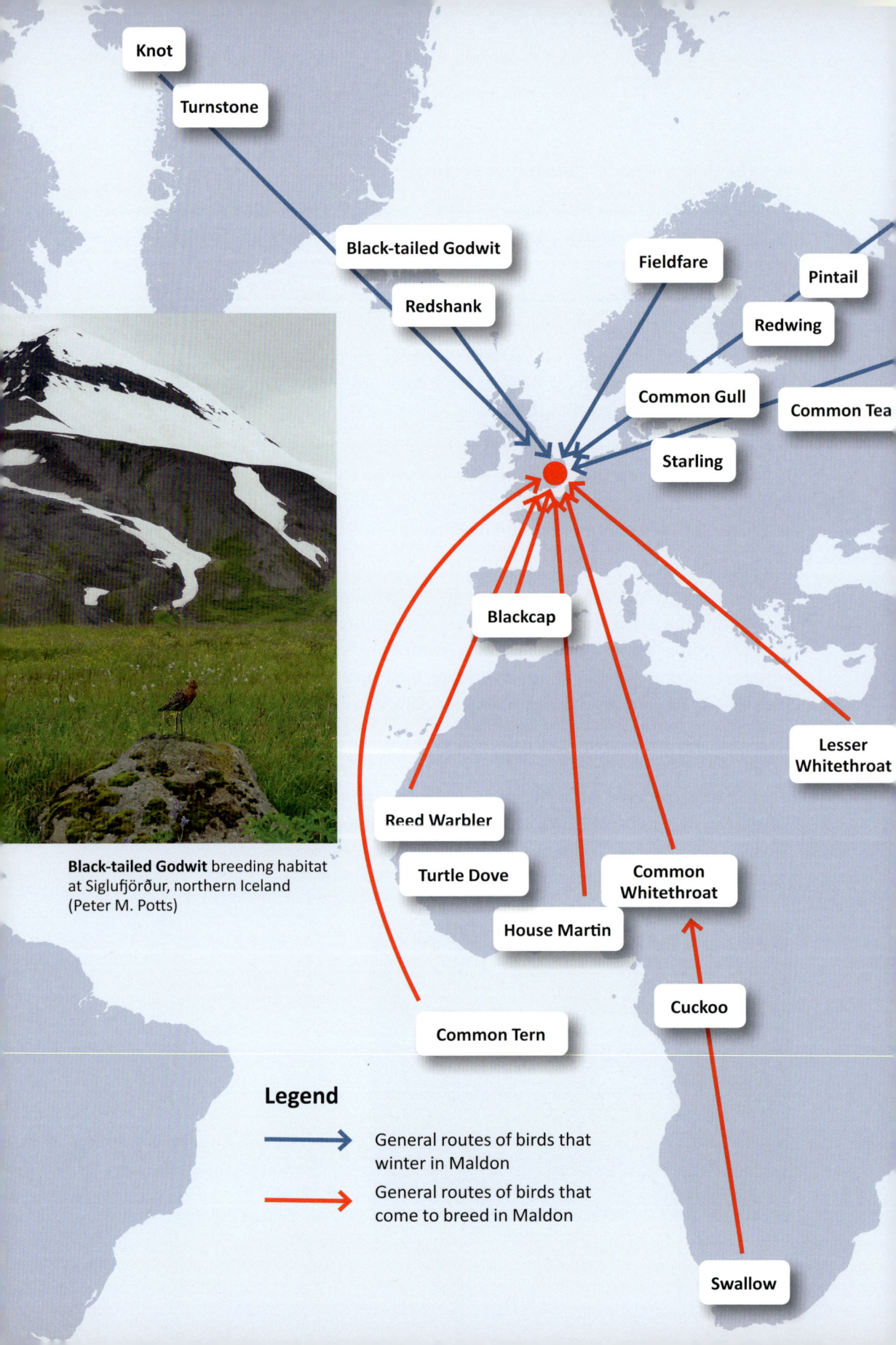

Knot

Turnstone

Black-tailed Godwit

Redshank

Fieldfare

Pintail

Redwing

Common Gull

Common Tea

Starling

Blackcap

Lesser
Whitethroat

Reed Warbler

Turtle Dove

Common
Whitethroat

House Martin

Cuckoo

Common Tern

Swallow

Black-tailed Godwit breeding habitat
at Siglufjörður, northern Iceland
(Peter M. Potts)

Legend

→ General routes of birds that
winter in Maldon

→ General routes of birds that
come to breed in Maldon

Brent Goose

Grey Plover

Wigeon

Dark-bellied Brent Goose on nest, Pyasina Delta, western Taimyr, Siberia (Barwoilt Ebbinge Research Team)

Flight Lines to Maldon

Annual migration routes taken by some of the area's regular summer and winter visitors

House Martin wintering in Mole National Park, Ghana (Graham Ekins)

Changing Patterns — Cycles within Cycles

To fully understand what species can be seen when around Maldon, the subject of the next part of this book, it is helpful to consider how occurrence and behaviour of the animals and plants we are watching is being driven by a whole complex of natural rhythms.

Day and night, the tidal cycle, seasonal changes and year on year climatic variations each exert their own influences. In turn there are also biological rhythms — breeding cycles and the cycle of life and death — and the interactions between populations of predators and prey.

In Maldon, it is the changing of the seasons and the rise and fall of the tides that make the most difference to what will be seen on any one visit.

On a longer time-scale, climate change is having an increasing influence on our flora and fauna. Even without human assistance, climate change happens as part of the natural rhythm of the planet. Humans have been fortunate that the last 10,000 years have seen a remarkably stable climate and it is quite possible that without that stability we may not have become as successful as a species as we have. There are now signs that the stability is coming to an end. Greatly exacerbated by man's proven influence, temperatures are warming at a pace not seen for tens of thousands of years and there will clearly be significant impacts on the planet's flora and fauna.

As will be seen in later chapters, global warming is already affecting Maldon's wildlife, with both winners and losers. Little Egret are perhaps the most obvious new colonists but there has been northward range expansion of a wide range of other species too, from gulls to damselflies.

Little Egret, Heybridge Pits, Feb 2016 (SW)

5
WILDLIFE THROUGH THE YEAR
(with a focus on birds)

WINTER

We start with the season when the weather may be cold, and many people prefer to stay indoors, but the number of birds around Maldon is at a peak. After donning the necessary extra layers of clothing there is no better way to immerse yourself in timeless wildness than to head east along the sea wall in the depths of winter. If you are lucky, you can walk for miles without seeing another person, surrounded instead by the sounds of Brent Geese, the sight of swirling flocks of Golden Plover and the smells of the tidal mud.

Wintering wildfowl on the estuary

At low tide, there can be thousands of birds feeding on the mud or loafing by the edge of the river. These numbers mainly comprise species of wader and wildfowl whose breeding areas are too cold or frozen over in winter to provide them with year-round sustenance.

The loudest and most obvious are probably the Brent Geese, arriving here from Arctic Russia. Breeding success of Brent Geese fluctuates wildly from year to year and the numbers reaching Essex vary accordingly. They normally arrive with their immediate families, the juveniles being recognisable by the pale-edged feathering of their wing coverts (the feathers that form the main panel of the wing). In some autumns, each pair of adults can arrive with two or more youngsters, while in other years there may be only a couple of young in every hundred. Populations of all birds and mammals breeding in the tundra zone are notoriously dynamic and are linked to the success of the Siberian Lemming, the preferred prey of the predators. In good lemming years, owls and foxes have plenty to eat and will leave the young geese alone. In lean years, the geese become more important as a food source and most of the goslings are taken.

Family party of Brent Geese, Southey Creek, Dec 2020: adult pair with three youngsters (JB)

When they first appear each year, the Brent are wary, but as winter progresses they become more relaxed and often allow close approach. No doubt this is due in part to Brent not being on the legal quarry list for wildfowlers! Historically, Brent had a very specific diet, eating Eelgrass growing in the tidal zone. To the frustration of farmers, in more recent times they have learned to feed on agricultural crops in fields adjoining the sea wall. Farmers along the Blackwater have tried various tactics to protect their crops, from scarecrows to replaying tape recordings of distressed geese, but all to limited effect.

Parties of Brent wintering at Maldon move back and forth around the estuary and

Two drake Wigeon and a drake Pintail along Colliers Reach, Jan 2021 (JB)

adjoining farmland, between favoured sites for feeding and resting, returning periodically to the river to have a drink and a wash. Birds interchange between other flocks wintering on the Blackwater and beyond, so the number seen on any particular day can vary considerably. When disturbed they will fly up with a lot of fuss. Their cacophonous gabbling forms the bass section of the winter soundscape.

The next layer of sound is provided by the dabbling ducks, so called because they feed at or just below the water's surface, rather than diving as many other ducks do. Large numbers of Common Teal feed by the water's edge. Common Teal are our smallest duck and next to Mallard, are the most widespread along the river, with some as far upstream as Beeleigh. They enjoy feeding in the creeks and wander over the mud in a similar way to the often-accompanying Redshank. There are lesser numbers of Wigeon, yet they can be more obvious, due to their characteristic whistling cry and the prominent white patches on their wings when flying.

The Mallard that arrive for the winter are often wilder and warier than their resident, park-loving cousins, though no doubt some of them quickly learn to copy the habit of eating bread when it suits them! Downstream by Northey and Osea Islands, small parties of Pintail are to be found. Pintail are the most elegant of this quartet and seem more reserved, having to be picked out rather than forcing themselves onto your consciousness.

In previous decades, a decoy at nearby Abberton was used to trap and ring large numbers of duck. Recovery of rings has revealed the likely origins of many of our wintering ducks — most come from North Eastern Europe and Russia, with some of the Wigeon and Pintail travelling the furthest.

The estuary also hosts large numbers of wintering Common Shelduck — winter peak counts around Northey Island have usually been over 500. In Feb 2013, over a thousand were counted.

A host of waders

Large numbers of wading birds also choose the estuary at Maldon as their winter home.

Each species has its own habits: preferred feeding styles, foraging areas and flocking behaviour. Redshank, ever noisy, the 'wardens of the marsh', really enjoy the mud. They spread themselves over the flats, probing with their medium-sized bills. In contrast, the smaller Dunlin keep in small parties, scurrying like mice, taking titbits from the surface. All are dwarfed by the Curlew that strut around searching for their favourite quarry: small crabs and worms.

Curlew, Colliers Reach, Jan 2021 (JB)

The birds with the most effective feeding strategies are those that can afford to spend long periods loafing about. Golden Plover are a case in point. Every year a flock of 500 or more build up and spend hours just standing together on the mud and shingle near the end of the Prom. They mostly feed on fields, often at night when their large eyes help them to pick out earthworms and beetles.

If you see a cloud of waders, high above the Prom it is likely to be these Goldies. It might be a sign of a Peregrine in the area, these plovers rank amongst their favourite quarry. If you don't see them you might at least hear them — their whistling calls are the top-end of the estuary choir.

Adding to the diversity, smaller numbers of a range of other species can also be found regularly amongst the estuary wader community. A cousin of the Golden, the Grey Plover is one of our longest distance travellers. They are more solitary when feeding, though they group together in flocks further down the estuary when roosting. They have the best, haunting call, conjuring up the wildness of their tundra breeding lands in Arctic Russia.

Turnstone particularly like spots with seaweed and shingle that they can root about in. The edge of the causeway to Northey Island is a favoured site. Turnstone are known for their extraordinary range in diet and often appear quite tame. For several

Flock of Avocet, off Heybridge Pits, Feb 2016 (SW)

years there was a small wintering flock around the quayside that were happy to feed on bread that had been thrown to the ducks and gulls.

In stark contrast to the varying browns and greys of most waders, there is now a regular wintering flock of Avocet. These birds are a relatively recent arrival on the Maldon scene. Each winter numbers have grown with a record 530 being seen in March 2016. Their preferred location changes each year. Sometimes they have frequented the river further downstream towards Maylandsea but increasingly they are spending their time at Maldon, visible along the edge of the river from the end of the Prom. A number are colour ringed and it seems they arrive here from a mixture of locations, from Northern England, East Anglia and from just across the English Channel.

A walk along the northern sea wall by the Osea causeway will demonstrate how, from the birds' perspective, different areas of mud hold different attractions. Knot and Bar-tailed Godwit have been relatively scarce towards Maldon but occur in numbers on the flats around the Osea Causeway. Oystercatcher too are commoner there — no doubt the available menu of shellfish and worms is subtly different and more to their suiting. A lack of sandy beaches must be the main reason for the lack of Sanderling records, with just two seen in the patch over the last decade.

Special mention must be made of the Greenshank. Only a handful winter in the patch but their distinctive 'tyu tyu tyu' call stands out from the background of Redshank calls, echoing across the estuary and alerting birdwatchers to look out for this more elegant bird, flying over the marsh with trailing legs and white rump contrasting against dark wings.

High tide

Twice daily, the rising tide completely transforms the estuary. As the river becomes navigable, the Thames barges are able to follow smaller vessels and dinghies in heading out from the quays. For the wading birds however, the change is less welcome. As water begins to immerse their feeding grounds they must seek sanctuary until it ebbs.

Where they go depends on the height of the tide and the level of disturbance. There are some mounds of spoil from river dredging that birds often congregate on which can be viewed from the sea wall at the western end of Heybridge Pits and by the recycling centre. Black-tailed Godwit roost on the spits and islands of Heybridge Pits. However the greatest numbers of waders roost on the salt marshes around Northey Island and on both sides of the estuary opposite Osea Island.

Avocets have a unique approach in that they are comfortable swimming — they sometimes choose to gather in tightly knit rafts when the water is not too choppy.

Black-tailed Godwits gathering to roost at Heybridge Pits (with Redshank), Apr 2016 (SW)

All these birds would be able to sit out the high tide in peace were it not for the wide variety of disturbances they have to contend with. When they errupt into flight it is often due to river traffic or dogs off the lead but it may be due to the presence of an avian predator — a Sparrowhawk or Peregrine or perhaps a Marsh Harrier.

Feeding time for those that swim...

For birdwatchers, the high tide is not all bad news as in winter a variety of waterbirds may follow the tide upriver into the patch to feed, pursuing their different strategies, whether chasing fish under the surface or diving down to feed on what's on the submerged estuary bed.

Regulars are Cormorant, Great Crested Grebe and Goldeneye. The Goldeneye are often in small flocks which are worth checking as there are occasionally individuals of other species such as Long-tailed Duck and Smew amongst them. Small numbers of Red-breasted Merganser winter and there can be the odd Common Scoter, Eider or Scaup as well.

Red-throated Diver, Heybridge Pits, Nov 2017 (SW)
Normally seen only distantly out on the estuary, this individual gave great views at Heybridge Pits

The stately Great Northern Diver is a rare treat. A few winter each year on the Blackwater though, along with Slavonian Grebe, they normally stay further downstream towards Goldhanger where there is permanent water. However this emperor of the bird world has on occasion been seen on Colliers Reach or even off Heybridge Pits, diving for crabs on the riverbed. To see one always makes a day special.

The best vantage points require a long walk, whether from Maldon along the sea wall to the sluice and beyond or the equally long walk from Mill Beach to the causeway to Osea Island. However, the lure of what might be seen is enough to encourage the effort, especially in poor weather, on the basis that this will encourage birds that normally stay downstream to head up river for shelter.

Normally the result of these endeavours is disappointment but occasionally there is good luck. On one memorable day on a bird race, in January 2009, we arrived at Osea causeway to find both a Great Northern and a Black-throated Diver as well as a Slavonian Grebe and two Long-tailed Duck all riding the rising tide — a great collection this far up river.

Gulls

As winter beckons, large numbers of smaller gulls, Black-headed and Common, arrive in the area. They are gregarious, often in mixed flocks and are most obvious on fields — farm fields, playing fields and parks — where they feed during the day. They are looking for worms and other invertebrates and are always on the lookout for fields recently worked by farmers where the surface has been broken up by ploughing or harrowing. Towards dusk, they head to the river, along with hundreds if not thousands of others from much further afield, to roost on the open water between Northey and Osea Islands.

The Black-headed Gull that come to spend the winter in Essex come from a wide range of different European countries, from Finland to the Netherlands, demonstrated by reading the numbers on rings that they have on them. The individual in the photograph has been seen in the Prom Park each winter since 2017, having been ringed as an adult in the breeding season at a colony at Świnoujście in Poland in 2016.

Since the closing of Maldon's open rubbish tip, the majority of the Herring Gull and Lesser Black-blacked Gull now wintering on the estuary are likely to be locally breeding birds. They are joined by a few hulking Great Black-backed Gull from

Polish-ringed Black-headed Gull, Prom Park, Jan 2021 (JB)

Scandinavia and the Baltic that stake out favoured patches along the edge of the water. Some of the Herring Gull must also come from further north — occasional birds show features of the larger Scandinavian *argentatus* race, slightly greyer on the back with whiter wing-tips.

The lack of flocks of bigger gulls means the chances of seeing rarer species caught up with them is low, however it is worth looking out for Yellow-legged Gull — in past years individuals have over-wintered in the area.

Saltmarsh passerines

The saltmarsh provides great habitat for wintering passerines, with food available from the seed heads of saltmarsh plants and from the invertebrates dwelling amongst the vegetation and muddy channels. A number of families are represented — larks

(Skylark), pipits (Meadow and Rock), buntings (Reed and Corn) and finches (Linnet and Goldfinch). Most of these birds roam generally over the adjacent farmland as well, often in small flocks, the exception being the more solitary Rock Pipit. Our wintering Rock Pipit are of the Scandinavian race *litoralis* and they very much favour the shoreline.

Flocks of Corn Bunting by the sea wall along the south of the river by Southey Creek have numbered up to 200 birds. Corn Bunting are very much a declining breeding species across the country, with Essex being one of the last strongholds, so wintering flocks are of key importance. The British population is thought to have reduced by 90% between 1970 and 2010.

In the past there may well have been regular flocks of Twite but, as elsewhere in East Anglia, Twite are now very scarce around Maldon, only being seen on a handful of occasions during the study period. A small flock present in January 2004 included some birds with colour rings that showed they had come from a breeding area in the southern Pennines near Burnley.

Raptors

The sizeable numbers of waders and passerines provide an obvious attraction to wintering raptors. A passing Sparrowhawk will put up all the plovers and smaller waders. If all the birds in the estuary take to the air it is likely that a Peregrine is on the hunt. Over the last decade Peregrine have become established as a regular sight, most likely a reflection of their increasing national breeding population. A look through a telescope at the end of Northey Island will often reveal one perched on a rock, scanning the surrounding area and planning its next sortie.

Peregrine, Southey Creek, Jan 2015 (SW)

The anticipation of seeing birds of prey adds excitement to any winter walk along the sea wall. Kestrel are the commonest predator along the river, hovering above the sea wall and field margins in their search for small mammals. They share habits with Barn Owl, which hunt similar prey. They are both resident, with some increase in numbers in winter due to an increase in young birds and a level of dispersion. Sadly Barn Owl are rarer but the ghostly vision of one floating over the marshes and along the borrow dykes is always special.

← Short-eared Owl, Heybridge Pits, Mar 2016 (SP)

↓ ' Ring-tail' Hen Harrier, Limbourne Creek, Oct 2011 (SP)

It is something of a lottery each year as to which other species may be seen. A Marsh Harrier is quite likely, a Short-eared Owl is a possibility. Both species are regular winterers. A combination of good numbers of voles in Scandinavia during their breeding season along with favourable winds during migration can deliver multiple Short-eared Owl. They particularly like the area around Limbourne Creek and have often roosted in the rough grassland there.

Less dependable, and hence making a day special, would be a sighting of a Hen Harrier or Merlin. There are currently so few Hen Harrier breeding in England that those seen must come from much further afield. Most of the Hen Harriers seen are the brown plumaged, bar-tailed birds — 'ring-tails' — which are young birds or maybe older females.

Occasionally however, perseverance may be rewarded by a sighting of a pristine adult male — pale grey, white rump, wings tipped in black with an elegance unmatched.

Along the tidal river and the canal

The stretch of river between the estuary and Beeleigh is relatively undisturbed and has its own set of winter residents, including a hundred or more Common Teal and a regular gathering of Little Grebe. Redshank and Moorhen frequent the edges and there have been wintering Common Sandpiper. It was here that a drake American Green-winged Teal was found in 2012.

In winter, Common Snipe arrive in numbers and are generally found along the margins of river and tidal pools. They tend to favour particular spots, often unseen until flushed at close range at which point they zig-zag up skywards calling stridently, "cretch cretch"...

Inland water

Regular watching has produced records of a variety of other duck species, the provenance of which is often hard to ascertain. The Ferruginous Duck seen at Heybridge Pits and Chigborough in 2005 was accepted as a wild bird from Eastern Europe but the various records of Red-crested Pochard, a common bird in collections, are most likely either escapes or perhaps strays from one of the increasing feral populations such as the one at Hanningfield Reservoir.

Another interesting duck found was a hybrid Mallard x Gadwall that turned up with a large arrival of Gadwall late in 2009 — these distinctive birds were in the past thought by some to be a separate species and given the name 'Brewer's Duck'.

Drake Green-winged Teal (with Common Teal on left), River Blackwater, Feb 2012 (SP)

Drake Ferruginous Duck, (with drake Gadwall on left), Chigborough Jan 2005 (RN)

Drake 'Brewer's Duck' (with female Gadwall), Chigborough, Dec 2009 (RN)

Different areas of water can attract different species. It is not always apparent what subtleties are involved though factors no doubt include water depth, prey species/food availability, area of open water and level of disturbance.

Goosander are very faithful to particular wintering sites — unfortunately, for no clear reason, there are no regular flocks within the Maldon patch despite the similarity of a number of sites to those that are frequented elsewhere. There is a traditional site just to the west, at Ulting, where double figure counts are regular. From here, birds do fly out to other waters to feed and so not surprisingly occasional birds are seen in our area, particularly at Ricketts Mere which is just a mile and a half away from it.

Regular watching has produced winter records of a variety of other duck species, such as Goldeneye and Scaup. There have been records of rarer grebes as well. During the winter of 2002–03 a Red-necked Grebe spent several weeks on the main lake at Lofts Farm and at one point was joined by a Slavonian Grebe.

The shrubs and small trees of waterside margins, such as the willow scrub at Chigborough, harbour sufficient insects to attract parties of tits and occasional wintering Chiffchaff. Regularly heard, though rarely seen, are Cetti's Warbler and Water Rail, the latter lurking mainly within the reeds but occasionally to be spied creeping about on open mud or even swimming from one patch of cover to another.

In winter, Kingfisher are more widespread and time spent around Chigborough and Lofts Farm will often be rewarded by sightings of one darting rapidly past, two-tone in azure and orange, signalled by its high pitched insistent call.

Kingfisher, Heybridge Lock, Jan 2017 (SP)

At Heybridge Pits, where there are beds of reeds and reedmace, there is a regular wintering party of Bearded Tit — a prize quarry for photographers due to both their looks and antics.

While a few pairs of Egyptian Goose now breed in the area, increasing numbers now roost on the pits suggesting they fly in from much wider afield for the night (44 of them in November 2016).

The main local feral geese, Greylag and Canada, can often be seen at Chigborough and Lofts Farm Lakes and around the surrounding fields. In winter they move in bigger flocks, often making a great racket as they commute to Heybridge Pits and the estuary.

These flocks are always worth checking as they can attract other visiting geese that are looking for company. These tourists comprise quite a mix. Some, like the occasional Bar-headed Geese, are likely escapes from collections.

↑ Bearded Tit, Heybridge Pits, Jan 2016 (SP)
← Tundra Bean Goose (with feral Greylag), Heybridge Pits, Oct 2016 (JB)

Others, such as Barnacle Geese, are of unknown origin as there are some quite large populations of feral birds breeding in East Anglia. Nevertheless, there are some that have the arrival patterns and behaviour to provide them with convincing wild credentials such as White-fronted Geese of the Russian race and, on two occasions, Bean Geese from the Russian tundra.

Distinctive-looking geese have proven that there is some movement of birds between Chigborough and Abberton Reservoir. Examples of birds seen in both locations include a colour-ringed (and assumed escaped) Red-breasted Goose and a hybrid Barnacle x Canada Goose.

Farmland

A wide range of species choose to winter on the farmland around Maldon, with flocks seeking out suitable fields for feeding and roosting. Food may be less plentiful than on the mudflats but there is no interference from the tide. The choice of field depends on the ground state and food preference. Golden Plover, Lapwing, corvids and winter thrushes are on the hunt for worms and other invertebrates, while geese and pigeons seek out more vegetative fare. The largest flocks are those of Woodpigeon, which can number hundreds. In amongst them, groups of their less conspicuous cousin the Stock Dove can often be found.

Common and Black-headed Gull also favour fields for feeding, their flocks often attracting larger gulls as well as the occasional Mediterranean Gull.

Many of the various winter flocks are nomadic, travelling in search of fields offering the best chance of food. Where there are seeds around, finches and buntings can be found. Modern farming is tidier than it was in the past, with less spilt grain. Nevertheless farmyards, such as those at South House Farm and Mundon Hall, are worth checking with House Sparrow, Chaffinch and Greenfinch regular, Yellowhammer and Reed Bunting frequent and always a chance of a Brambling.

Field hedgerows can contain a mixture of fruiting plants and in good years can be berry-laden in winter, with sloes, haws and rose hips. These attract thrushes — Blackbird, Fieldfare and Redwing. The hedges also provide safe vantage points for these and other species such as finches that also feed on the ground. Excitable flocks will fly back and forth as their dominant drive alternates between hunger and fear of attack.

Field ditches are worth checking as they can attract Common Snipe and Green Sandpiper and very occasionally a Jack Snipe, though the ratio of birds seen to miles walked may be low!

In areas where there are Pheasant shoots, farmers often sow strips of maize, millet and other game crops for the food and cover they provide for the Pheasant. These can prove a magnet for finches and buntings, in particular Linnet, Goldfinch and Chaffinch. Mixed flocks have included Lesser Redpoll, Greenfinch and Reed Bunting along with occasional more unusual species such as Brambling. In January 2016, one such

Jack Snipe, Heybridge, Feb 2012 (JB)

area of game cover off Chigborough Road attracted hundreds of birds including some Common Redpoll and also a Merlin that was taking advantage of the increased concentration of potential prey.

Woodland

In winter, woodland birding is a completely different experience to that of spring or summer. The lack of foliage can mean a good view and yet it might seem there is little to see as the summer visitors have flown south and other species have dispersed to farmland and gardens in their quest for food.

It is worth persevering to seek out mixed flocks of foraging birds. Tits predominate: Great, Blue and Long-tailed. Coal Tits too, where they occur, generally on the western side of our patch. The Tits may be joined by Treecreeper and Goldcrest, an overwintering Chiffchaff, or even Firecrest, a species that is an increasing winter visitor to Essex.

Damp woodland is used for daytime roosting by wintering Woodcock. In good years for them, be ready for an explosion of feathers if you inadvertently flush one from the leaf litter close to your path. Jays can be very obvious as they noisily roam the woods for acorns and it can be a good time to see Great Spotted Woodpecker.

Firecrest, Mill Beach, Jan 2019 (SW)

Towards dusk, as birds start heading to roost, an air of excitement can build up as a wood fills with contact calls. It is worth following up on alarm calls as birds may have found a Tawny Owl, perched close against the trunk of an old tree amongst the ivy. Indeed in wintertime Tawny Owl themselves can be quite vociferous as they call to confirm the boundaries of their territories, with younger birds trying to stake out their own areas amongst the established territories of mature birds.

Gardens

As elsewhere in the country, Maldon's gardens play a major role in supporting bird populations through the winter. This is both a consequence of homeowners growing plants for their own enjoyment and increasingly taking pleasure in providing food especially for their avian guests.

The range of birds found is generally similar to that found elsewhere in the county. In 2015 the RSPB's Big Garden Birdwatch identified the top twelve garden birds in Essex as shown at right.

This ranking looks good for Maldon with the caveats that Collared Dove is currently the commoner dove (though Woodpigeon are increasing within the town) and Goldfinch is probably now the commonest finch, with Chaffinch having experienced a worrying decline in the last five years or so.

Just outside the RSPB top twelve was Long-tailed Tit but it is moving up the chart, reflecting its increasing numbers — it's a species that seems to cope well with human presence and is learning to use bird feeders.

The top twelve garden birds in Essex	
1	House Sparrow
2	Starling
3	Blue Tit
4	Blackbird
5	Woodpigeon
6	Collared Dove
7	Great Tit
8	Robin
9	Magpie
10	Chaffinch
11	Goldfinch
12	Dunnock

Sadly Greenfinch and Song Thrush are both less common in gardens than they once were. The former possibly due to the spread of *trichomoniasis*, a disease born by parasite first noted in garden birds nationally in 2006, the latter to a reduction in garden snails and other invertebrates due to use of chemical pesticides in gardens and further afield.

Fortunately, one bird found perennially in Maldon's gardens is the Robin. Confirmed as Britain's National Bird by popular vote in 2015, it remains the quintessential garden companion and Christmas cover star. The Robin's plaintive winter song is the natural voice of the season.

There is no doubt that birds become accustomed to visiting gardens and using bird feeders. Goldfinch are now familiar in gardens, particularly where Nyger seed is provided. At certain times of year, two other finches, Siskin and Lesser Redpoll, may also be seen. They are both winter visitors and traditionally feed on the seeds of smaller trees such as alder and birch, species it is pleasing to find amongst the landscaping of newer housing estates. The latest recruit to the Maldon garden scene is Reed Bunting. Near to wetland areas, such as Heybridge Pits, it too has learnt to use garden feeders. Regular watching can occasionally provide sightings of scarcer visitors to the bird table, including Brambling and Common Redpoll. In December 2019 Simon Wood's diligence in keeping his seed hoppers topped up was rewarded by the appearance of a Tree Sparrow, the first to be seen around Maldon for some years.

Male Reed Bunting on feeder in Simon Wood's Heybridge garden, Feb 2018 (SW)

Blackbird and other thrushes come to gardens to feed on berries, particularly in bad weather. While Blackbird may be seen all year round, many of those seen in winter are not our resident birds but visitors from Scandinavia. Redwing also come from Scandinavia. They stand out as being somewhat distinctive, with pale stripes over their eyes and red flanks and underwings. If you have apples on offer then you may attract Fieldfare. These big thrushes can be quite aggressive, chasing away other species that show an interest in 'their' food.

All of the birds that we spend our time encouraging into our gardens do in turn become an attraction to Sparrowhawk. A walk through Maldon will often reveal one or two soaring above housing areas and many have had the experience of one whooshing by on a low level pass through the garden and, when successful, flying off with a victim from the bird table. If doves are caught, they are often too heavy to easily take away and so in these instances, a hawk may be seen plucking its prey in full view on the lawn, surrounded by a cloud of feathers.

Fieldfare, Maldon garden, Feb 2021 (JB). They tend to turn to gardens in hard weather, when the ground out in the fields is too frozen for them to dig out worms

Gardens provide a sheltered microclimate that can form a welcome wintering site for some less usual species. Most warblers migrate to Southern Europe and Africa for the winter, however gardens in Maldon now host a number of wintering Blackcap each year. Another bird seen benefitting was the smart male Black Redstart whose wintering territory for 2010/11 included John Buchanan's back garden in Mariners Way.

Winter roosts

As daylight fades the winter sky above Maldon fills up with birds heading to their roosts. The most obvious are corvids, Rook, Carrion Crow and Jackdaw, streaming high overhead, heading from the farmland that they have been feeding on towards their favoured night-time quarters. Traditionally they have used woods to the south of the district but increasingly over our study period, large numbers of Jackdaw have begun roosting in trees at the back of Chigborough Lakes. It is difficult to count them but in Oct 2020 we estimated 1500 may have been present, with their strident "chyack-chyack" calls causing a commotion that rings out over the surrounding countryside. The best place to view the Chigborough roost is from the gate on Scraley Road. Other species to be seen arriving here on a winter's evening include Magpie, Fieldfare and Blackbird. It is also a good place to watch for Woodcock, which roost

Jackdaw and other corvids at Chigborough Lakes roost site, Oct 2020 (JB)

in the damp woodland during the day, as they head out for a night shift foraging for worms in nearby fields.

There are no long-established large Starling roosts in the area, though every so often temporary roosts can form to suit as foraging birds pass through the area. The biggest roost we have seen, of up to 5,000 birds, has been in the reeds around the back lakes at Chigborough. It remains to be seen whether this develops into a regular site for them. Even when roosting in small numbers, Starling are good to watch, as they perform small scale versions of the much televised murmurations of hundreds of thousands of birds that occur elsewhere in the country.

Wetland reedbeds and similar vegetation are also sought out as roost sites by pipits and buntings. Thick wooded areas and bushes are used by thrushes. Pied Wagtail have the confidence to seek out warmth around human environments including streetlights and heated buildings, the retail area by Morrisons and the roof of the swimming pool being good examples.

Different wintering strategies

Not all birds coming to Maldon to winter have travelled a long distance. Changes in food availability and increased competition from high post-breeding populations can drive local dispersal. Winter habitat needs are less exacting than in the spring and summer, when suitable nesting sites are needed. In Maldon, Kingfisher appear around the estuary during the winter months and Grey Wagtail can be seen in a wide variety of wet and muddy locations away from their breeding sites along rivers and canals, occasionally even visiting garden ponds.

Bearded Tit are another good example of this phenomenon. During the study period, a small party wintered annually at Heybridge Pits. It is likely that these are birds that breed in the larger reedbeds to be found elsewhere in East Anglia. In the case of Bearded Tit, they often use their winter travels to find new breeding sites — we suspect that they may indeed have bred at Heybridge Pits in recent years.

Migration strategies evolve. The aforementioned Blackcap that now winter in the UK are different birds to those that arrive each spring to breed here. They have been shown by ringing studies to be birds from breeding populations in central Europe, which are now flying west to winter in the UK rather than heading south to winter around the Mediterranean. The other 'summer' warbler that is found wintering regularly around Maldon is the Chiffchaff. Again the wintering birds come from somewhere else but exactly where from is still to be discovered!

Male Blackcap, Maldon Town, Jan 2010 (SP)

Another strategy entirely is followed by the Water Pipit. They breed in the Alps and other mountain ranges in Southern Europe. They are altitudinal migrants, seeking out low level areas to escape the winter snow and ice. This flight from a harsh environment leads some to travel north to the UK each year. Occasional birds have been found by coastal pools and dykes around Maldon and it appears that there is a small wintering population here. Individuals have been seen by Mundon Wash, along the sea wall by Osea and at Heybridge Pits.

Water Pipit, Heybridge Pits, Feb 2016 (SP)

Cold weather movements

Cold weather on the continent can drive large numbers of birds across the North Sea in search of frost-free feeding grounds. Skylark, Lapwing and Woodpigeon can be the most obvious as they head south-west over the town. Woodcock may drop in and be found in unexpected places, such as one that turned up in a garden in the south of the town. In the cold snap of Jan 2010 there were sightings of Woodcock all around Maldon.

Large numbers of wildfowl may also be involved in these movements and some years these have included small parties of Bewick's Swan and grey geese — Pink-footed and White-fronted. In December 2020 there was a big influx of White-fronted Goose from the near continent into South-East England. Our share included a flock of thirty eight that spent a few days in fields along Southey Creek.

Whooper (left) and Bewick's Swan, Southey Creek, Jan 2013 (Tom Harris)

If Maldon freezes it is bad news for local birds. Many move out of the area entirely, Little Egret often being amongst the first to leave.

As inland waters ice up, ducks seek out remaining patches of open water and many move to the estuary. Ornamental ducks can be frozen out of private ponds, such as the time when three California Wood Duck turned up at Chigborough Lakes. Many waders concentrate around the edge of the river while Water Rail can turn up in the smallest of ponds. It is worth checking any water that is still free-flowing water such as the Lime Brook where it cuts across the fields south of Limebrook Way.

Bittern at Slough House Farm, Dec 2010 (SP)

Bittern have also turned up, from the continent or possibly from elsewhere in the UK where, thanks to the RSPB, its population rose during the final decades of the 20th century from being virtually extinct to being a regular breeder in numerous reserves.

In these tough times, garden feeding stations can be life-saving for struggling woodland species. In hardest weather, birds become desperate, forced to forsake their natural timidity. J. A. Baker, the Chelmsford-based author of '*The Peregrine*', graphically described finding birds succumbing to the cold during the exceptional winter of 1962/3. Fortunately for the local wildlife, winters since have not been so cold.

Charismatic winter visitors

Smew, Chigborough Lakes, Feb 2008 (RN)

Certain species have a combination of looks, character and scarcity that give them a special appeal. In cold winters the occasional Smew can turn up. These are small ducks from northern Scandinavia that always seem to have an energy that stands out. The females and young birds are known as red-heads however the prize is to spy the exquisite drakes — named 'white nuns' by 17th century naturalist John Ray on account of their white hoods. Although seen in flocks on the continent they are usually seen here as individuals or in parties of two or three. Lofts Farm and Heybridge Pits are the prime sites around Maldon. During our study period the record count was at the former with 2 drakes and 8 red-heads together in February 2012.

For many, especially photographers, *the* target Christmas bird is the Waxwing. They are known as an irruptive species and flocks arrive in numbers into the UK when

Waxwing, Maldon, Dec 2010 (SP)

a successful breeding season coincides with a poor berry crop in Scandinavia and Russia. Even in good years only a few thousand may be seen throughout the whole of the country. However, they have favoured haunts and fortunately for us, Maldon is one of them. Particularly large numbers arrived in the winter of 2010/11 when up to 130 were seen here during what has so far been the biggest invasion that Essex has experienced. Famously fond of petrol stations and supermarkets due to their tendency to plant cotoneaster and other berry laden bushes, Morrisons by the A414 roundabout has been our number one site.

Great Grey Shrike, Heybridge, Oct 2015 (SP)

Mention must also be made of the Heybridge Great Grey Shrike. Found by Simon Wood in October 2015 it stayed the whole of the winter through to March and was a fantastic bird to see. Its presence, coinciding with that of Bearded Tit and a very photogenic Short-eared Owl, generated a significant increase in interest in Heybridge Pits amongst local nature fans and camera buffs which has maintained its momentum as evidenced by continued postings in the Friends of Heybridge Gravel Pits Facebook site.

In 2010 we had a brief visit from a Snow Bunting. This bird was unusually tame, indicating that it may have come from so far north that it was not used to human presence. Oct 2010 (SP)

A winter highlight at the end of 2020 was the appearance of parties of Russian White-fronted Goose that had arrived from the continent. Here are four that were found in a field just to the east of Limbourne Creek, Dec 2020 (JB)

SPRING

Harbingers

Whilst a few Snowdrop and Crocus may start flowering in January it is generally February before the natural signs of spring begin to appear. Everyone has their own set of indicators they look for to signal the end of winter. It may be the appearance of different catkins, the first frogspawn or the emergence of queen bumblebees, bumbling about in their search for nesting sites. Brown Hare begin chasing around fields along the sea wall, with the jills turning and boxing to fend off the advances of the amorous jacks.

The first birds singing are resident species, keen to get things going before the competition arrives from the south. Great Tit can seem to be all over the place, with their 'tee-cher' cries, while Song Thrush and Blackbird contribute with their more mellifluous melodies. Bright sunny days will encourage Skylark to ascend high above the fields and pour forth their far-carrying songs — perhaps the classic sound of the English countryside?

Cawing Rook begin their nest-building in the treetops overlooking the car park at Morrisons, while in woodland, the sound of Great Spotted Woodpecker drumming adds background percussion. Woodpigeon are early nesters as are the Cormorant and Grey Heron that start to spend more time in the trees at Chigborough.

King of the early songbirds is the Mistle Thrush, holding forth from the tops of isolated trees, seeming to bare his soul with his wild and mournful stanzas.

Other bird families use other methods to woo potential mates. Wintering ducks come into full breeding plumage at the start of the year and begin courting in early spring. Goldeneye throw their heads right back to impress the ducks, while for Common Teal it is more of a contest, as several suitors gather round lone females, each flicking their heads to attract attention. Mallard drakes seem to quickly become bored with displaying and resort to the less subtle approach of simply chasing the ducks until they submit.

The most developed displays are those of the Great Crested Grebe. Their famous penguin dance can be seen where they breed at Chigborough Lakes, Heybridge Pits and other lakes. Both birds dive down to collect some weed and then swim back to each other and then stand up in the water face to face to present their offerings in a head-shaking ritual.

Male Great Crested Grebe in 'cat display', a precursor to the 'penguin dance', whilst a third bird watches, Home Water, Feb 2021 (JB)

Raptors demonstrate their prowess through their flying skills. On a warm spring day, it is often possible to watch Sparrowhawk soaring in display above suitable wooded breeding sites and increasingly over recent years, Common Buzzard as well. One year we were lucky enough to watch Marsh Harrier skydancing over the reedbed by Osea Causeway.

Blossom and early flowers

Throughout residential areas, from late February, cultivated cherry trees begin to burst into blossom to proclaim the arrival of the new season. Along hedgerows, Blackthorn starts the display with the mayflowers of Hawthorn bushes joining in a few weeks later, lining the roads with their massed white petals. A wide variety of wild plums, damsons and other fruit trees add their part too to the promise of longer and sunnier days ahead, though in some years, cold blasts of weather from the east can arrive to postpone these initial hopes. There can be significant consequences if blossom is delayed as there are many insects whose own lifecycles depend on early availability of nectar.

Primrose begin flowering in damp shady spots while the first woodland flowers include the strong yellows of Lesser Celandine and the whites of Wood Anemone. Red Dead-nettle appear along path edges. Timing of first occurrences has been gathered annually by the Woodland Trust since 2000 from observers throughout the country. Results clearly demonstrate the impact of climate — in some years, warm weather has encouraged many of the flowers being recorded to appear three weeks earlier than in other years.

Wheatear, Heybridge Pits, May 2015 (SW)

First of the migrants

On to March 1st, St David's Day, heralded by early daffodils and it's time to look out for the first of the returning migrants. Chiffchaff and Blackcap are normally the first to be heard, though as occasional individuals of both species winter around Maldon it can be uncertain if early singers are newly arrived or not. During this period, there are often sightings of finches, Siskin, Lesser Redpoll and Brambling, that are passing through on their way back to northern and continental breeding sites.

The best places to search for the first certain summer migrants are Lofts Farm/Chigborough Lakes and the sea walls. The former for Sand Martin, the earliest of the hirundines, which may be spotted hawking low over the water for an insect snack to sustain them on their way north. The sea walls are a good bet for an early morning Wheatear. Males, in their spic summer plumage, look specially dressed for the new season, as they flit up from the ground to a perch from which to view their temporary surroundings. Both these species are termed passage migrants — they do not breed locally but pass through, triggering speculation as to just where they may be travelling to. The Wheatear are likely headed for some hilly moorland in the north of Britain or beyond.

Soon Chiffchaff and Blackcap will be arriving in numbers and the first Swallow will appear, maybe spotted perched on a roadside telegraph wire. One by one the other migrants arrive and there is a certain amount of anxiousness as you hope they all return from their travels. It is amazing to think of the thousands of miles they have flown since they were last in Maldon. Gradually different habitats fill up. Sedge Warbler pop up in reedbed scrub, Common Whitethroat in field hedgerows and Common Tern patrol the river. A walk around Heybridge or along the sea wall to Limbourne early on a spring morning offers a good chance of hearing the first Cuckoo in the second week of April.

When weather fronts hold passage up, large numbers of Swallow and martins can gather at Lofts Farm and Chigborough — this is often a great time to look for Hobby. Looking like snappier, more streamlined Peregrine, these falcons are nimble enough to prey on them and are a delight to watch. They are the one true summer migrant from amongst our falcons though sadly they do not regularly breed around Maldon.

Hobby, Chigborough Lakes, May 2010 (SP)

Spring waders

On the estuary, the behaviour of the waders begins to change. Many of the species that have wintered begin to gather in tighter flocks as they contemplate heading off on their migrations with Golden Plover being one of the first to go. Numbers of Black-tailed Godwit initially increase as Maldon forms a staging post for birds that have wintered further south and west. Well over a thousand can be seen and they gradually change their plumage tones from brown and grey to the orange of their summer dress. As the days pass, there is a sense of excitement amongst the Redshank and Godwit as they prepare to leave (termed "Zugenruhe", restlessness for travel, by German ornithologists) until each group picks its moment, calls increasingly and swiftly climbs up high to fly off back to Iceland. To see this happen, and to imagine the journey these birds are undertaking, is a wonderful experience.

Whimbrel, off Heybridge Pits, Apr 2016 (SW)

The patch also forms an important staging post for Whimbrel, the smaller cousin of the Curlew, with numbers peaking around early May. During one bird race we counted over 30 spread around various muddy spots from Osea to Southey. Known also as the 'seven whistler' owing to their distinctive repeated call, they are often heard before they are seen as they fly by.

Many of the passage waders have already assumed full summer plumage, making them an attractive sight to look out for. The non-descript Dunlin gain black bellies and rufous backs while Bar-tailed Godwit and Knot both change from greyish hues to brick-orange body feathering. Turnstone have chestnut backs and a strikingly patterned black and white head and breast. One of the latest to moult but most impressive of all is the Grey Plover that develops a black face, breast and belly, edged with white and contrasting with a wonderfully spangly silver crown, nape and back.

Smaller numbers of other waders pass through, including Common Sandpiper and Greenshank. Occasional Little Ringed Plover are spotted but as they favour the gravelly edges of lakes they are readily disturbed and generally move on — during our study period they only bred in one year, in 2007 at Heybridge Pits.

Nightingale and Turtle Dove

As the season progresses, the longer distance migrants arrive, including the Nightingale. John Keats captured the magic when he portrayed the Nightingale as the Dryad, the tree spirit, that "in some melodious plot of beechen green and shadows numberless, singest of summer in full-throated ease".

Nationally it is very much a declining species so we are very lucky to still have Nightingale around Maldon. The main stronghold over the last few years has been at Hazeleigh Wood where over a dozen singing males have been counted but there are usually further individuals at Chigborough and along the canal by Langford. When good numbers return from Africa there may be additional birds, with males heard in recent years from Heybridge Pits, Maldon Wick and Elms Farm Park, but the overall trend is worrying with less than 20 pairs currently within the patch.

They first appear during the 2nd–3rd week of April and while they do sing during the day to establish territories, it is at night their voices really stand out when there is little background noise and they reach out to the heavens to attract prospecting females.

Some people say they prefer the songs of other species, such as those of the Blackbird or Skylark, but even so the Nightingale's remains unchallenged for its power and control.

Another declining iconic species that is still just holding on in the patch is the Turtle Dove. Hearing the gentle purring song is a relief each year, showing that once again at least

Nightingale, Hazeleigh Wood, May 2021 (SW)

Turtle Dove, Heybridge Pits, June 2011 (SW)

some have managed to literally dodge the bullets during their long return migration. They are smaller and quicker than other doves and not always easy to see but a good view is a pleasure. Again Chigborough is a good site, with other birds occurring along the canal and odd birds in past years at Heybridge and around South House Farm.

The full dawn chorus

Here in the UK we have some of the world's best birdsong (compensating for the relatively dull plumage of our birds compared with avifaunas elsewhere). Most of the main players can be heard around Maldon, making it well worth setting the alarm and getting up early to listen to them.

A good place to go is Chigborough, where the background sounds from the waterbirds add an extra dimension to the experience.

Arrive well before dawn on a calm morning in early May and the first sounds you hear may be the hoot of a Tawny Owl or the crowing of a distant Pheasant. Then the resident birds will start up, Robin, Song Thrush, Wren. Next will be the warblers. Chiffchaff, Blackcap, Common and Lesser Whitethroat. Reedbeds and wet scrub can provide Cetti's, Reed and Sedge Warbler and knowing where to find them can deliver Willow Warbler and Garden Warbler as well. On one occasion we also caught up with a Grasshopper Warbler — ten singing warbler species in one day!

Add in Cuckoo, a selection of finches and with luck a Nightingale and it can be a bit overwhelming — time for a well-earned breakfast!

The last of the wintering birds

It can seem surprising that while all around the breeding season is in full swing, there are still some wintering birds that have yet to head off.

Out on the estuary, Brent Goose, Grey Plover and Bar-tailed Godwit may be seen well into May. The reason they linger is that these are species that breed in the high Arctic. They need to delay their departure to be sure that their destination will have thawed before they reach it. The geese are usually the last to leave, with some staying on almost to the end of the month.

Spring surprises

As the season progresses, there is always the chance of seeing more unusual migrants just passing through. Garganey is an example, the only duck that is a summer migrant to the UK. It is scarce and secretive but occasional pairs have been sighted at Chigborough and Lofts Farm. Another is Osprey — single birds sometimes pause to try their luck plunging for fish in the estuary on their way perhaps

Drake Garganey, Chigborough Lakes, May 2012 (SW)

to a breeding site by a Scottish Loch. On an April morning in 2003, Simon Patient had a surprise when he encountered a White Stork circling above him at Lofts Farm.

Winds from an easterly direction can drift birds towards us that were heading up the North Sea. Black Tern and Little Gull are cases in point with both occurring almost annually within the patch. Heybridge Pits and Lofts Farm are good places to look as these species mainly feed by flying over areas of open water and dipping down to pick edible items from the surface.

Damp cropped grass around cattle or horses, as at South House Farm and Lofts Farm, is worth checking for continental races of wagtails. White and Blue-headed may be sometimes be spotted in amongst parties of the more familiar Pied and Yellow Wagtail.

Another traveller to look out for is the Greenland race of Wheatear. They are a bigger bird than their European relatives and the males in springtime can have a lovely

Ring Ouzel, Limbourne Creek, May 2011 (SP)

peachy wash to their breasts. Their longer wings have evolved to carry them far to the north to their Arctic breeding sites.

In May 2011, a continued period of easterly air delivered a bumper crop of spring migrants to the patch, no doubt aiming originally for Scandinavia. The highlights included a male Ring Ouzel at Limbourne, and both a Common Redstart and, even better, a Wryneck at Lofts Farm. During this same purple patch, a Nightjar was seen along the canal towards Langford, perhaps on route to breeding haunts in the East Anglian Brecks.

A few years later, in April 2020, another sustained easterly airflow coincided with the Coronavirus lock down. It was a strange time for all of us. Along with almost everyone, we were restricted to our gardens for most of the day. Happily though we had superb weather, ideal for thermals, and we were treated to an unprecedented passage of raptors overhead. Depending on flight lines and location, some observers scored more than others. The overall tally between 4th April and 10th May included numerous Sparrowhawk, dozens of Common Buzzard, a double figure total of Red Kite and at least four Osprey! Other species seen were Marsh Harrier, Peregrine, Hobby and Kestrel. Topping the bill were three majestic Common Crane.

Common Crane, Maldon, April 2020 (JB)

They were picked up by Nick Lindsell as they arrived from the east, completed a circuit of South Maldon and then headed off north-west. Had John Buchanan not been working from home due to lock down he would have missed the awesome sight of them passing over his house!

The one that got away was a White-tailed Eagle from the Isle of Wight reintroduction scheme. Satellite tracking subsequently showed that it had passed through our air space near Langford but failed to be spotted by any local birders.

Late arrivals

Late in the season there can be a final pulse of arrivals. These may include one or two Turtle Dove and also Reed Warbler, the latter often turning up in unusual locations as if they are struggling to find vacant territories elsewhere. The first singing Reed Warbler at the revamped Marine Lake in the Prom Park arrived late in the season in 2010 — now they are established as a regular breeding species there.

Finally, all the birds that have made it safely back from their wintering quarters are settling in and hoping for good weather over the coming weeks as they begin nest building and raising their families.

SUMMER

The June solstice, when the day is longest and the sun at its highest, signals that summer is upon us. Most species are already fully immersed in breeding activity, hoping to capitalise on the peak of food availability.

Birds are at their busiest, with success hinging on weather, temperature and the insect crop. Different strategies are used, with many having large or multiple broods to make the most of it when times are good. These are often the species that have high mortality in winter and so need the ability to recover quickly. Many time their broods to match the hatching of specific prey, such as Blue Tits that hope to be able to feast on the usually abundant oak-feeding tortrix moth caterpillars.

Woodlands become full of the high-pitched calls from young birds, particularly from large families of tits that are searching the foliage for sustenance.

Summer at the Pits

The noisiest activity is around the Black-headed Gull colony at Heybridge Pits. There is a constant racket with seemingly every individual bird calling at maximum volume with contact and alarm calls from the adults while the youngsters keep clamouring to be fed. There are frequent skirmishes as the larger Herring and Lesser Black-backed

Black-headed Gull colony, Heybridge Pits, June 2012 (SW)

Gulls from the industrial estate seek to carry off and devour any unattended chicks. More outnumbered, the smaller number of Common Tern try to defend their own families from all of the gulls. Somehow a few succeed each year. You can almost sense the adults relaxing once the chicks are old enough to properly defend themselves.

The reedbeds are the summer home to Reed Warbler. Some years more than forty singing males have been counted around the pits, along with lesser numbers of Sedge Warbler and Reed Bunting. Besides competing with their brethren for nest sites and food, these three all run an additional risk, being known host species to Cuckoo, one or two of which can usually be heard or seen.

In 2016 there was an explosion in numbers of Brown-tail Moth caterpillars. Most bushes were festooned with their silk-spun nests and more than a few people ended up with rashes following contact with their toxic hairs. The caterpillars did however prove a hugely popular feast for Cuckoo, attracting at least seven to the pits. With a great deal of calling, and birds flying back and forth over the lakes, they became a great attraction for visiting birders.

Cuckoo, Heybridge Pits, Apr 2015 (Tom Harris)

Heron Central

Just to the north at Chig-borough Lakes, a cacophony of croaks and gurgling emanates from the heronry within the Essex Wildlife Trust reserve. Grey Heron and Cormorant begin nesting first and take the prime positions. The Little Egret arrive later by which time the foliage has grown and considering they are all white they can be quite hidden within the trees. All three species are resplendent

Heronry at Chigborough Lakes EWT Reserve with nesting Cormorant, Little Egret and Grey Heron, June 2021 (JB)

in their mating plumage. The Cormorant grow white plumes around head and neck, particularly prominent on older individuals and even more so on those with continental ancestry. The bills of Grey Heron become bright yellow with a pink base and their crests and breast feathers reach peak condition. Meanwhile the Little Egret grow their 'aigrettes', the long plumes of upper breast and recurved scapular feathers that in the past adorned the heads of 'fashionable' ladies, a tradition that was thankfully ended by the campaigning women who formed the society that was to become the Royal Society for the Protection of Birds.

Summer on the saltmarsh

Once the wintering birds have left, the saltmarsh can seem quite bereft of birds. It nevertheless has its own breeding specialities — Redshank, Oystercatcher and Meadow Pipit (though it looks as though we have now lost Meadow Pipit as a breeder). The yodelling song flight of Redshank and parachuting display of the Meadow Pipit have been characteristic sounds in early summer. Oystercatcher are the noisiest as they display and bicker and fly overhead with seemingly incessant piping. These 'Oiks' often choose oddball nest sites — they have tried nesting in a depression on top of one of the fence posts along the Northey island causeway and on top of a mooring post off the Prom. Indeed one year a pair delayed refurbishment works of the Prom itself when they chose to nest in a cavity on the sea wall.

Common Shelduck often nest inland and so can be seen commuting back and forth to feeding sites along the estuary. They generally raise their families by the coast so face the challenging task of marching their ducklings cross-country to the river.

Common Shelduck have a somewhat unorthodox approach to parenting. Different broods of ducklings are gathered into 'crèches' that can number twenty or more youngsters, to be looked after by those adults with the strongest parenting instincts. The rest of the adults undertake a 'moult migration' whereby they head off to the Wadden Sea off the coasts of the Netherlands and Germany where they join a hundred thousand other Shelduck from all over northwestern Europe for their late summer moult. A couple of times we have encountered Ruddy Shelduck along Southey Creek. It is quite possible that these are birds from the continent that have become caught up with our Common Shelduck returning from the Wadden Sea.

Parklife

In summer the Prom Park becomes a bustling hub of human activity with people arriving from all over Essex to enjoy everything ranging from kite flying to car shows.

A hungry Starling waiting to be fed, Prom Park, Apr 2004 (JB)

Wildlife will always try and take advantage of a situation and anyone who sits down by one of the cafés or starts eating from a bag of chips will soon attract the attentions of Starling and gulls. The majority of the gulls will be Black-headed Gull, many from the colony across the river at Heybridge Pits. The ducks are always hungry too and a ready crowd of Mallard and Coot will appear before anyone throwing food out to them at the Marine Lake (the adjacent café sells cups of grain for this very purpose).

Once the crowds leave in the evening, the grassy car parks and football pitches clear, providing feeding grounds for families of Pied Wagtail and rest areas for the gulls.

Mute Swans

Without doubt the most noted individual birds in Maldon are the swans of the Prom Park. Ever since the Marine Lake was re-landscaped into an ornamental pond, a pair of Mute Swan has nested there. They are well fed by visitors to the park but

'Polish' Mute Swan cygnet (2nd from right), Beeleigh, July 2010 (JB)

nevertheless do not always have an easy life as they have had past run-ins with Fox and errant pet dogs. Friends of the swans have taken to posting updates on their progress each year. Mute Swan also nest on most of the larger lakes around Maldon and also along the river and canal. Indeed a pair along the canal managed to successfully raise a family of eleven cygnets in 2019.

Both in the Prom Park and at Beeleigh, we have seen examples of the 'Polish' variant, a result of a genetic pigment aberration which causes cygnets to be born pure white rather than the usual grey. Adult Polish swans have pinky-grey feet. (They are thought to be known as 'Polish' due to birds showing this trait being imported into London from the Polish Baltic Coast in the early 18th century.)

City centre screamers

Although often confused with swallows and martins, Swift are special. Their lives are amazing in that they only land when nesting. Otherwise, they are permanently in flight — feeding, mating, and even sleeping on the wing. They can be high flying, their narrow black scythe wings showing as punctuation marks against the clouds.

A great feature of summer around the High Street is when parties of Swift rush by screaming as a breeding display and as unpaired birds seek partners. Nationally numbers are reducing due to the reduction in insect life and in nest sites but fortunately in Maldon there are still old buildings providing suitable roof top cavities. One of the best places to look for them is above St Peter's Hospital.

Swift travel very long distances to feed. When there is a hatch of insects, large numbers of Swift can gather, with Heybridge Pits and Lofts Farm occasionally attracting large frenzies of birds in the right conditions.

Beeleigh Falls

The walk along to the weir and falls at Beeleigh is always enjoyable. Check along the water's edge for Grey Wagtail hunting for insects — this has been the one place they breed around Maldon. Look out also for Kingfisher too, their sharp high pitched 'zee(t)' call signalling their presence as they flash by.

If you head further along the canal you may hear a variety of warblers, including Garden Warbler on occasion, as well as a possibility of Nightingale or Turtle Dove.

Owls

We are fortunate to have several different species of owl regularly breeding around Maldon.

Grey Wagtail, Beeleigh, May 2016 (SW)

Tawny Owl, the wise brown owl of literature, hold territories where there are big trees with large enough holes to nest in. Their far-carrying tremulous hoots can be heard from a number of older wooded areas, such as Mundon Furze, Hazeleigh Wood, Maldon Wick, along the canal, around Langford and at Chigborough. They are essentially nocturnal. It takes luck to spot one roosting during the day, typically sat on a thick branch amongst ivy, tucked in against a tree trunk. The best clue to their presence may well be the excited mobbing calls from small birds that have discovered them first.

Barn Owl are birds of open countryside and have bred in all compass points around Maldon. Like Kestrel, Barn Owl will use nest boxes and have done so where they have been provided at Osea and along Southey Creek. Their numbers are very sensitive to the prevailing weather. Rain can prevent them hunting while prolonged cold means reduced numbers of voles and other prey species.

Barn Owl, Osea Road, May 2013 (SW)

They are fantastic birds to watch as they flap, glide, twist and turn on silent ghostly wings, hunting along field edges, borrow dykes and saltmarsh. Although most often seen in the evening or in the lights of headlamps at night, when hunger or the demands of parenthood dictate they may hunt in broad daylight.

Little Owl are farmland birds. Although they hunt at twilight they can be often be seen by day and are best looked for perched in trees by their traditional nest sites. They have a variety of calls but can be unobtrusive. Regular haunts have included Lofts Farm, along Scraley Road and around Mundon and they have also been seen along Fambridge Road and at the back of Hazeleigh.

Recent study work by Adrian Dally has proved that a fourth species of owl is also breeding locally — Long-eared Owl. Generally nocturnal and inconspicuous, they are best located by calls, particularly the distinctive 'squeaky gate' call of the owlets. Adrian has located a couple of nesting locations around Mundon. Occasional individuals have been seen in daylight, including one a number of us watched in May 2013 hunting along the sea wall by Southey Creek.

Summer oddments

Sometimes the unexpected can show up. It may be birds that should have left after the winter but have stayed around, whether through injury or lack of migration urge. We have seen a Brent Goose in July and in 2014 a young male Goosander decided to spend the summer on the river as it came of age.

One particularly unpredictable species, with a unique lifestyle, is Quail. Our smallest and only migrant game bird, they have a very short breeding cycle and can breed in waves as they travel north from Africa in late spring. Some of the youngsters from first broods are able to mature quickly enough to breed later in the same year.

At least three times in our study period, Quail made it to Maldon. Unfortunately, they frequent crops that are taller than they are and are rarely seen but they do have a distinctive, far carrying song which allows them to be found. In each case they were in fields to the south of the town.

When birds are not enough!

In high summer, birds become less obvious as they sing less and are busying themselves looking after their young. At this time, many birdwatchers turn their attention to the emergence of butterflies and dragonflies. There is much to be said for them — they are colourful, relatively easy to spot and prefer sunny weather!

Maldon Wick EWT Reserve is great for a wide variety of species. Skippers and Common Blue butterflies frolic within the meadow area (where we have also found Bee Orchid). Emperor and Brown Hawker dragonflies patrol over the pond, while around the edges there are Black-tailed Skimmer and damselflies — several different blues, including Small Red-eyed, as well as Common Emerald and, more recently, Willow Emerald too. Along the old railway there are Speckled Wood and Ringlet butterflies and both Purple and White-letter Hairstreak.

Another good walk on a summer's day is along the canal at Beeleigh. Along the edges, Banded Demoiselle flutter in the sunlight, the males with black patches on their wings that seem to flicker as they fly while the wings of the females shine with green iridescence. It is now a regular site for Scarce Chaser dragonflies, their presence being an indicator of good water quality in the canal.

More butterflies can be seen along the sea wall amongst the clovers and thistles, particularly along the path following the south side of the river by Northey Island. Meadow Brown, Gatekeeper and Small Heath can be seen as well as

Banded Demoiselle on a Yellow Water Lily, Beeleigh, July 2018 (JB)

different whites. The sea walls are also good for day-flying moths, the most noticeable being Cinnabar and Narrow-bordered Five-spot and Six-Spot Burnet, and the more cryptically coloured Mother Shipton.

Growing the right plants can attract some of the most colourful butterflies into your own garden. Throughout the built-up areas of Maldon and Heybridge, Buddleia bushes bring in Red Admiral, Small Tortoiseshell and Peacock and, in years that are good for immigration from the continent, Painted Lady as well.

Gardens often harbour large ant colonies, the ants choosing to build their nests in the sand lying under patios and block paving. These swarm when large numbers of flying males and queens emerge on their nuptial flights. These are often synchronized so that many colonies emerge on the same day, creating clouds of ants busy mating, with the queens then seeking out locations to begin new colonies. These clouds form a bounty for those birds that can take advantage. Flocks of Black-headed Gull and Starling gyrating above a housing estate are a sure sign that this is happening.

Small Tortoiseshell, Heybridge Pits, Apr 2013 (JB). (Sadly a species currently in decline)

Dependent on date and weather, mass hatches of other insects can occur, creating feeding frenzies amongst those that prey on them. The most well-known are mayflies, which emerge over the canal in late May or June and provide welcome sustenance for hungry fish. But there are also a host of assorted gnats and midges that can do so as well as caddisflies. The narrow pathways around the lakes at Lofts Farm and Chigborough can be surrounded by dense clouds — fortunately most of them do not bite us humans!

Signs of changing seasons

Different species follow different calendars and it is not long before some are ready to transition to the next chapter in their lives. While some are still raising their second, even third broods — House Martin are sometimes still feeding chicks in September — others seemingly can't wait to leave us!

Adult Cuckoo are amongst the first to depart and may already be back in Africa while their progeny are still being fostered. It is simply amazing that the youngsters, migrating later, somehow make it to Africa and back without ever having met their biological parents! Swift leave early too, to carry on their epic travels. Meanwhile other birds that have bred in northern lands will be starting to arrive back in Maldon.

Female Green Sandpiper can be the first to arrive back from their breeding sites in wooded marshes in Scandinavia. They have a domestic arrangement whereby the females generally leave their mate behind to look after the chicks on his own. The Dump Pool and Heybridge Pits are good places to look for them. On one occasion

Russell Neave saw a still northbound Wheatear and a returning Green Sandpiper on the same day, a rare conjunction of spring and autumn migrations.

July is a month for dispersal from breeding sites to areas looking for new feeding opportunities and perhaps to explore potential future breeding locations. Families of Starling gather together in large flocks that can be seen around the farms along the river and on the saltmarsh. Black-headed Gull arrive from many different directions. The apparently uniform flocks appearing on fields and along the river may contain birds from the Low Countries and North Sea and Baltic coasts as well as from colonies in the UK. Yellow-legged Gull, the southern cousin of the Herring Gull, also disperse into South East England from the continent. In the early 2000s odd individuals could regularly be expected to be encountered off the Prom and along Southey Creek with as many as ten being seen in July 2003. They have recently become scarcer. Perhaps as less food waste now ends up on open rubbish tips, the attraction to cross the English Channel to visit us has diminished.

Families of terns also disperse. Little and Sandwich Tern unfortunately do not nest around Maldon although they do breed further out along the Blackwater and most years odd individuals and occasional family groups turn up to take advantage of fishing opportunities in the estuary.

Around this same time, Curlew begin to appear and, in the evening, can be heard calling as they circle over the town. Other waders also trickle down. Mostly adults that have failed to breed successfully, they have cut their losses and headed south early. These can include the first returning Black-tailed Godwit. Careful scanning of the saltmarsh may reveal Lapwing or even an early Whimbrel.

As we hope for sunny weather for final barbecues, wasps switch from hunting invertebrates to feed their grubs to seeking out sugary food for themselves and home

in on any unattended drinks and plates of food that we might be trying to enjoy outdoors. There will still be some dragonflies about, Migrant Hawker and Common and Ruddy Darters, and it seems too soon to accept the inevitable. But reluctantly we will have to admit it. Summer is drawing to a close. Autumn has arrived.

Ruddy Darter, Maldon Wick, Aug 2020 (JB)

AUTUMN

Autumn is a time of change and preparation for the winter. Animals must take every opportunity to build up fat reserves and migrant species need to travel in search of places likely to offer a greater chance of survival. Visually the landscape changes as leaves change colour and drop. With the increase in plantings of non-native trees such as cherries, maples and sycamores, there can be spots around the town where there are sufficient yellows, oranges and reds to match the kaleidoscope of the famed North American fall. In our older woods, some of our native trees do provide more colour, though there are not enough of them to create a landscape scale effect.

Autumn is also characterised by our two main harvests: the grain harvest, so vital for the making of bread (and beer!), followed by the harvest season for fruit. Our forefathers recognised their importance, celebrating them with festivals, their lives being wholly linked to the rhythm of the seasons. For many insect and bird species, the success of the fruit crop is crucial, some species adjusting their diets to take advantage of the bounty, many warblers eating berries to build up energy prior to migrating.

Post breeding season, bird populations are at their highest. Families of tits exemplify this. Parents can be seen busily foraging in bushes and trees with large numbers of

The autumn palette in Hazeleigh Wood is enriched by the reds of Wild Service Tree and the yellows of Field Maple

youngsters in tow with often 4 or 5 or more in a family, all keeping together with their incessant high-pitched contact calls. These large broods are insurance against the struggle they will face over the coming months — most will not survive to the following year.

Locally, the avian biomass is further boosted by the release of hundreds if not thousands of Pheasants that have been raised over previous weeks ready for the shooting season. Sadly for them they lack the survival skills to cope with the automobile so many escape the gun only to meet their end on our roads.

General exodus

As our migrant breeders slip away to begin their southerly journeys, they join a general exodus of birds from the UK. This is when passage migrants can be seen — birds from other parts of the country that pass through Maldon on their way to their wintering grounds. The most obvious are hirundines, Swallow and Sand Martin, often to be seen hawking for insects over areas of open water. For a few weeks over the end of August and the start of September they can often be watched towards dusk gathering in flocks at Heybridge Pits as they use the reedbed as a temporary roost site. After roosting overnight many will head off again on their migration in the morning. It is fascinating to consider the challenges they will face and the sites they will see along their journeys, through Europe, across the Mediterranean and on into the depths of Africa.

Whinchat, Limbourne Creek, Sept 2010 (SP). A few pass through Maldon most years

Most songbirds migrate through the night. Early in the morning, it is worth checking bushes and hedgerows for any birds that may have stopped off to spend the day resting and feeding up. Typical amongst these travellers are warblers, Chiffchaff, Lesser Whitethroat and Blackcap being the most commonly encountered.

Wheatear and Whinchat, both open country relatives of the Robin, are autumn regulars. Limbourne Creek is a favoured location but there is a chance to see either of them anywhere along the sea wall, Wheatear flying up from their ground-based search for food while Whinchat perch on the look-out from fence posts and tops of small bushes.

Certain weather conditions, such as clear skies early in the night followed by a bank of rain can force larger numbers of migrants to land to take shelter and regain their bearings. At these times less regular species may turn up. Over the years we have found a number of Spotted Flycatcher and Common Redstart around the patch. Some places seem to be particularly attractive to passing migrants. The bushes surrounding the main lake at Lofts Farm are a case in point. Perhaps the proximity of water attracts them as this signals the likely presence of insects for them to feed on. Willow Warbler and the odd Garden Warbler have been regular here in recent years plus good numbers of Common and Lesser Whitethroat. Frequent visits to Lofts Farm in August 2019 were rewarded by the finding of a couple of Pied Flycatcher, stopping off on their way south from northern Europe.

In the spring, migrants are driven to travel quickly to make the most of narrow windows of breeding opportunity. In contrast, the journey south is generally taken at a more leisurely pace, with birds often stopping with us for a few days to break their journeys, such as the Osprey that spent a fortnight along the river by Northey Island in October 2017.

Osprey, Southey Creek, Apr 2013 (Tom Harris). Always an exciting bird to see!

Wading birds from all directions

As autumn progresses, significant numbers of waders start arriving. Many of the first waves are from Iceland and Northern Europe — Black-tailed Godwit, Redshank and Golden Plover, along with smaller numbers of Greenshank. The latter tend to feed individually at the edge of the river but then gather to roost, often on a secluded spit or bank around the edge of Heybridge Pits where counts of over fifty have been made in recent autumns. Ruff and Spotted Redshank are much less frequent around Maldon, the latter less than annual, even though both are regular elsewhere in Essex. Maybe there is some subtlety in their habitat preferences that is missing locally or perhaps potential haunts have simply not been found by recent migrants and so not been handed on in the inherited memory to later generations in the way that some spots become regular stop off sites.

The first flocks of arriving Dunlin are of the *schinzi* north-west European race. They have relatively short bills and the adults are often still sporting their black belly summer plumage. They are joined by Ringed Plover and also parties of Turnstone. The next waves of species arrive from further afield, including flocks of longer-billed *alpina* race Dunlin, Grey Plover and Bar-tailed Godwit from Scandinavia and Northern Russia as well as Knot from Greenland and Arctic Canada. Close scrutiny of the Dunlin flocks can reveal the presence of juvenile Little Stint and Curlew Sandpiper. Usually only odd individuals of these are seen and are something of a reward for diligent observers. In a way they bracket the Dunlin. The Little Stint are smaller, with short, straight bills and scurry along as they feed (photo on page 224). Meanwhile Curlew Sandpiper stand taller than Dunlin with longer, down curving bills and a more elegant demeanour. Their identification is clinched if seen in flight and their white rumps seen. Curlew Sandpiper are truly long distance travellers, having reached us from breeding sites in Arctic Siberia and then continuing on to final wintering quarters in Africa, covering total distances of 15,000 km or more. Most years just one or two are seen locally but occasionally double figure counts are made — in September 2005 a flock of 26 was watched on the mud opposite the Dump.

Curlew Sandpiper, off Heybridge Pits, Oct 2017 (SW)

Incoming ducks

The first ducks to arrive are Common Teal, which can appear as early as July, at Chigborough, on Heybridge Pits and at the Dump Pool. Next, Shoveler and Gadwall arrive. Along with Mallard, at this time of year these ducks disport a wide range of plumages — adult males and females, different ages of immatures, and all in various stages of moult. Many of the adults are still in 'eclipse' plumage. Each year, adult ducks need to shed their flight feathers and replace them with fresh new feathers. To limit their risk during the vulnerable time when they are unable to fly strongly, they adopt a strategy of first replacing their bright body feathers with a drab 'eclipse' plumage. This leads to males looking similar to females as their new primary and secondary wing feathers grow through. Once the wings are in good condition, fresh body feathers are grown so that by late autumn the males are looking again like they are supposed to!

Many of the first wildfowl are migrating pre-emptively, to bag the best wintering sites or else refuelling while en route to more distant locales. Later arrivals, Wigeon, Pintail and Brent Goose, may be coming from further afield and waiting till they have been actively driven out by colder weather. When they reach us they behave quite timidly, keeping away from the sea wall — many of the first years may never have seen a human before! As the weeks progress they become more used to the movements and sounds of people and great views can be had from paths along the edge of the estuary.

Markers of the season

We each have specific sights that we look for each year to confirm that autumn is fully with us. For the birdwatcher it is often the return of species that come to Maldon to winter. It may be the Common Gull appearing amongst the flocks of Black-headed Gull or the first Great Black-backed Gull arriving from Norway. It could be the first flight of Wigeon arriving into the estuary or the gruff calls signalling the arrival of Brent Geese. A walk along the sea wall, which is by now turning muddy, may provide sightings of Rock Pipit along the water's edge or Common Snipe, flushed from the borrow dyke.

As the days shorten, there is a point when you begin to feel a chill in the air and a feeling that we have turned a corner. It is at this point

Redwing, South Maldon, Feb 2021 (JB)

that walking back from the pub, the steady high-pitched 'seep' calls of Redwing may be heard overhead. The first waves of these Scandinavian thrushes often fly straight over us as they head further south and west. Those birds that will winter with us tend to arrive a bit later, seeking out berry laden hedgerows and fields to search for worms and other invertebrates.

Visible and invisible travellers

Most species migrate nocturnally. As you lie in bed hundreds, maybe thousands, of birds could be travelling by high above you. They use various means to navigate including the moon and stars and, for some at least, the earth's magnetic fields. The peak of migration is often around the full moon when birds have the best chance to see something of the geography ahead of them to help fine tune their course. It can be somewhat frustrating to be thinking of the wonderful species that are passing over, out of sight.

Other species are more cooperative from a birdwatcher's point of view and migrate during daylight. These include pipits and finches. Skylark and Meadow Pipit call frequently and migrate on a broad front — they may be spotted flying purposefully anywhere over Maldon. Occasionally a longer, thinner call may draw attention to a Tree Pipit passing by. Migrating finches follow the coast. In the right conditions, a walk along the sea wall may be enhanced by the sight of small parties heading by. Knowledge of their calls can help in picking out Lesser Redpoll, Siskin and the odd Brambling amongst them.

Far more obvious are flocks of Starling and Woodpigeon, heading in from the continent. At times, flocks of the latter may number hundreds, if not thousands, to the dismay of many farmers...

Passing raptors

Birds of prey also migrate by day, often waiting for the sun's heat to generate thermals that they can use to help them gain height before they head off on the next leg of their travels. As noted earlier, the centre of town, with its buildings and position at the top of a hill, is particularly good for generating thermals, as is the line of woodland running along the higher land towards Great Totham. The most numerous of

Common Buzzard, Heybridge, Mar 2021 (JB)

these migrants are Common Buzzard and Sparrowhawk — sometimes several can be seen soaring together, forming a 'kettle' as they slowly swirl round in the thermals.

Drift migrants

Periods of easterly winds can mean that species travelling south over continental Europe may drift across the North Sea and be seen passing down the eastern edge of Britain. A classic example is the Honey Buzzard. A rare breeder in the UK, many thousands head south each autumn from Scandinavia to winter in equatorial Africa. In the right weather conditions they are worth looking out for and have been seen over Maldon in 2000 and 2009. One found at Maldon Wick by Nic Lindsell in August 2012 chose to break its journey here, spending the night in Hazeleigh Wood.

Another migrant that chose to break its journey here was the Spotted Crake found at the Dump Pool at the end of August in 2007. It ended up staying into September and showed very well to admirers from all over Essex and beyond.

Spotted Crake, Dump Pool, Sept 2007 (Andy Cook)

Stray seabirds

Generally seabirds passing Essex track the North Sea coast and, when visibility is good, they tend to cut straight across the mouths of the main estuaries — the Blackwater, the Crouch and the Thames. However there is always the chance that bad weather, or a misplaced sense of direction, may send occasional individuals up the River Blackwater to Maldon. It is always exciting to see birds designed for the rigours of the oceans appearing inland. Our sightings have included Gannet (an adult flew right over the Prom on a day so windy that parkrun was cancelled), Kittiwake (particularly on foggy mornings when lack of visibility has led them to hug the coast) and, on one occasion, a Fulmar gliding past three surprised observers at Osea Road.

Juvenile Gannet, Southey Creek, Oct 2012 (Tom Harris)

Skuas are amongst the most thrilling seabirds to see but sadly have only very rarely been seen around Maldon. There have been records of all four of the species regularly occurring around the UK, including Long-tailed Skua — in September 2011, Simon Wood spotted two juvenile Long-tails flying past the causeway at Osea, and watched them as they gained height over Northey Island and headed off south.

Skuas live piratically, chasing other birds to give up their own prey and at times scavenging on and even killing other birds. It is likely that many birds have an inherent fear of them. On one occasion Simon watched all the birds in the estuary rise up in panic when an Arctic Skua flew up the river past Heybridge Pits. Many of them had probably never seen a skua before!

Records of auks (the northern hemisphere's answer to penguins) have also been few and far between. Outside of the breeding season they tend to live their lives well out to sea. Occasionally though, as with other sea birds, odd individuals can be impacted by the weather and brought our way. During the study period, Guillemot turned up four times and twice, Little Auk. Little Auk are Starling-sized and breed in vast colonies around the arctic. One November day, Daryl Rhymes watched a no doubt confused Little Auk fly up the river to Heybridge Pits and then join with a party of Starlings to fly off inland over the Dump Pool. Sadly the only Puffin to have turned up was picked up sick at Osea Causeway in February 2003. It was cared for by Laura Cheskin, of Maldon Wildlife Rescue, but died on 5th November, quite possibly due to stress caused by the noise from fireworks set off that night.

Insects migrate as well

Perhaps surprisingly considering their size, quite a number of insects migrate here every year. Some, such as Painted Lady butterfly and Silver-Y moth are regular, while others, such as Hummingbird Hawk-moth are less frequent. All these three mentioned are garden visitors. Hawk-moths hover in front of flowers as they extract nectar using their long proboscis and can lead the uninitiated to think that they have indeed spotted a hummingbird!

Hummingbird Hawk-moth, Heybridge, June 2019 (SW)

Many insect migrants travel here after breeding though they may choose to breed if conditions are right. Their numbers here depend on breeding success but very much also on weather conditions, as favourable winds greatly assist their travels. At times the movements can be very impressive. In May 2009 there were large numbers of Painted Lady butterfly arriving across the country. John's notebook entry read: *"28 May: Around 10 am, first noticed Painted Ladies flying strongly and determinedly in a westerly direction across our back garden (in South Maldon) flying just above fence height. Some dawdled, but*

Painted Lady, Heybridge Pits, July 2016 (SW)

most kept going. Around 20 per hour in ones and twos. Fewer later but noticed on and off all day." If a hundred passed through one garden, there were likely to have been many thousands flying over Maldon that day.

Occasionally some species have a mass emergence on the continent and astonishing numbers arrive in the UK. Examples include 7-Spot Ladybird, Marmalade Hoverfly and Diamondback Moth, the latter a significant agricultural pest that arrived in enormous numbers in 2016 and seemed to be everywhere for a while.

Autumnal largesse

Whilst all these birds are arriving, departing and passing through, much of the countryside acts as a service station, providing a bounty of fruit for refuelling and places to rest up and recover from long flights. The arriving flocks of finches and thrushes seek out berries. Early in the season these include blackberries, haws, elderberries and sloes. Towards the end of the season the winter berries begin to appear — Ivy, Holly and Mistletoe.

In the Prom Park, the most obvious fruit are the conkers that drop from the avenues of Horse Chestnut. There are far more than are needed to satisfy the needs of the few children who still play conkers, however they tend to lie uneaten as they do not feature in the diet of the park's wildlife (in London parks it is said that the feral Ring-necked Parakeet do eat them). Much more popular are acorns. In autumn, Jay in particular roam away from their breeding areas looking for Oak trees and can be seen flying to and fro as they collect the acorns and bury them in the ground in favoured spots to provide sustenance during the winter.

Open season for fungi

As the majority of life seems to slow down towards winter, in amongst the rotting leaves on woodland floors, mushrooms and toadstools appear. Fungi are mysterious, neither plant nor animal. The mushrooms and toadstools are merely the fruiting bodies of organisms whose mycelia, their webs of thread-like hyphae through which they ingest their nutrients, can spread over wide areas, linking together and communicating with trees and other plant life. They play a key role in the decay of plant material to allow it to be regenerated to sustain future life.

Fungi can be seen throughout the year but it is in the autumn that they become most obvious as myriad forms make an appearance. Some may be found on the ground, in woods, on open grassland, in churchyards. Others grow in trees, dead or alive, often favouring specific timbers. Their whole demeanour seems to conjure up the spirit of the Samhain, the pagan festival celebrating the cycle of death and rebirth, and the notion that so many are poisonous, or can produce psychedelic visions, somehow seems fitting for the season. Their names play further into this mystique — Dead Man's Fingers, Amethyst Deceiver, Witches' Butter, Destroying Angel…

The fungi themselves can be fascinating to investigate. Surprisingly bright colours, different textures (from jelly to leather). Just don't touch, let alone taste, the unfamiliar — appearances with fungi can be very deceptive!

↑ Beefsteak Fungus, Hazeleigh Wood, Nov 2020 (JB)
↗ Stinkhorn, Hazeleigh Wood, Oct 2017 (SW)

↑ Magpie Inkcap, Hazeleigh Wood, Sept 2018 (SW)
↗ Chicken of the Woods, Prom Park, Sept 2020 (JB)

All Saints Church, at the top of Maldon High Street

View of 'The Downs', on the slope between the High Street and the River Chelmer (SW)

6
AVIAN RARITIES

When birdwatchers meet and ask each other "is there anything about?" they do not mean the question to be taken literally. Even on a quiet day around Maldon there are likely to be hundreds if not thousands of birds to be seen, especially if you look over the estuary. What they are really getting at, is to find out if anyone has seen anything unusual. A species seldom seen, or in numbers not usually encountered. The real prize is to see a "mega rarity" a bird hardly, if ever, seen before. Over the years we have been lucky to find a good number of "Maldon megas" — birds not previously recorded here.

The excitement comes from the satisfaction in finding the unusual amongst the commonplace, the challenge of successful identification and the realisation that what you are looking at is not being imagined — that you are finally in the company of a long sought after species. There is great enjoyment in experiencing the character of unfamiliar birds, in seeing details only previously read about in books and in thinking about the incredible journeys these avian travellers have undertaken to bring them to Maldon.

Of course very often a rare bird is first found by someone else. There is then the added tension of not knowing if you will get to it while it's still about, the anxious search and then the relief if you are in luck and it appears before you.

The current use of text pagers and messaging has been a mixed blessing for us. Whilst it has helped in sharing news and allowed us to see each other's finds, there have been times when we have been galled to hear about cracking birds when we have been detained at work or stuck in another part of the country, unable to reach them before they have flown off.

There are many different reasons why unusual species turn up. There often is no clear explanation and we cannot tell if their appearance is accidental or intentional. Are birds that are migrating in the wrong direction lost and have a faulty navigation system or are they pioneers, following an instinctive 'wanderlust' to discover fresh wintering areas? Have birds been caught up in bad weather or have they overshot their normal journey through simple over enthusiasm?

For many birdwatchers, autumn is the most exciting time. It offers the best chance

Spoonbill, Heybridge, Aug 2018 (JB)

Nic Lindsell found the first Spoonbill in recent times on the river while walking with his dog Fenn around Heybridge Pits. His phone call with the news caused John to drop his chopsticks in the middle of a Chinese meal and dash straight over, just managing to get there as light was failing. The Spoonbill fed energetically for a further half hour before flying off south, not to return.

of finding a rarity. There are millions of birds on the move, of which a very large proportion are immatures that haven't travelled before and so have instincts still to be honed by experience. However rare birds have been found in Maldon in all months and from all cardinal points. It is probably easiest to review some of Maldon's rarer visitors during our study period by considering their different origins and the circumstances that might have brought them here.

Southern overshoots

During the spring, southerly winds can encourage birds migrating north to the Mediterranean to keep on flying. Then, with luck, birds that you might normally associate with holidays in Southern Europe can turn up by the Blackwater. A good example is Red-rumped Swallow. Twice we have been lucky enough to see one when weather systems have encouraged large northward passages of our regular Barn Swallow and martins. Another classic overshooting species is the European Bee-eater — in May 2011 one flew high over Adrian Dally as he was counting waders by Mundon Creek. While all the rarities just mentioned did not hang around, the Black-winged Stilt that Nic Lindsell found at Limbourne Creek in 2013 was much more accommodating, giving great views as it strutted about on its surprisingly long pink legs.

Herons and their allies seem to have something of a pioneering spirit. Birds that have overshot seem in no hurry to return south and may spend years roaming around looking for places to their liking. The Glossy Ibis that was seen around Lofts Farm in March 2012 had a ring on it that confirmed it had hatched from an egg in Coto Donana in southern Spain but had then been sighted in South West Wales before

visiting us in Essex. The lakes around Chigborough have a great attraction for these wanderers, with Great White Egret being seen on several occasions, towering above their regular Little Egret cousins, and a visit from a Night Heron in June 2019.

Waders from the East

The habitats around Maldon are particularly attractive to waders and wildfowl and over recent years they have attracted a range of rare species. Waders are robust birds and survive well if weather systems and poor navigation lead them astray. Both Terek and Marsh Sandpipers breed in Eastern Europe and Russia

↑ Black-winged Stilt being harassed by a Black-headed Gull, Limbourne Creek, May 2013 (SP)

↗ Glossy Ibis, Chigborough Lakes, Mar 2012 (SP)

→ Marsh Sandpiper, Heybridge Pits, Aug 2008 (RN)

and normally take an overland southerly route to their wintering sites in Africa. We have been lucky to have seen both here, when weather systems have led stray individuals to appear alongside our more expected waders.

Caught up with the mob

Another reason for rarities turning up is when they meet up with other species that normally fly here and end up joining these birds on their journey to Maldon. One such example is the Black Brant, the race of Brent Goose that breeds in Eastern Siberia and normally flies towards Pacific coasts to winter. A few pairs breed amongst the easternmost breeding Dark-bellied Brent Geese and each year a small handful join the flocks of Dark-bellied Brent that journey to Essex. They are travelling in what is apparently completely the

Juvenile male Baikal Teal, Chigborough Lakes, Oct 2010 (Adrian Kettle)

An excellent find during one of our bird races, when we were trying to see as many species as possible during a day spent within the Maldon area. Unfortunately the bird did not stay long and, despite much searching, was not relocated subsequently.

wrong direction however they seem quite content and some return in successive years. Most winters one or two Black Brant are picked out amongst the Brent Geese around Maldon.

Similarly ducks sometimes get caught up with the movements of other 'carrier' species. In Oct 2010 a group of us were amazed to come across a 1st winter Baikal Teal in amongst a party of freshly arriving Wigeon at Chigborough Lakes. This was an incredibly rare bird in a UK context — only the third accepted record. As its name suggests, its origins are from the Far East. Lake Baikal is in Siberia, north of Mongolia. The main wintering sites for Baikal Teal are in Korea.

Visitors from America

Given Maldon's east coast location it may seem a surprising place to find birds from North America. However prevailing westerly winds, combined with the annual hurricane season, can disrupt the journeys of birds migrating between breeding sites in Canada and the States and wintering areas in Central and South America, bringing them over to Europe. Interestingly, a high proportion of the American vagrants seen around Maldon have been found in the spring. Perceived wisdom is that most American birds seen in Britain come over in the autumn, when there are a lot of inexperienced young birds travelling and the weather systems can be strongest. These will then hit land on the west coast, where sightings are highest, before in many cases continuing the journeys south to winter, maybe around the Mediterranean or in Africa. In the following spring these may head north on a broader front as they try to return to the latitudes they were raised in.

Again it is wader and wildfowl species that best survive these long journeys. Waders seen here include a Lesser Yellowlegs on the river off Heybridge Pits in March and April 2009. The Lesser Yellowlegs is an American equivalent of our Redshank, breeding in Canada and normally wintering in the West Indies and Central and South America. After spending a few days in Maldon, it is interesting to think about where it headed next, perhaps flying north and becoming confused as to why it was unable to find its breeding site. Vagrants of species that winter in more northerly latitudes in the US are more likely to winter in Europe if they end up over here. A good example is the Spotted Sandpiper seen at Heybridge Pits in December 2011.

At least two species of American duck have also made it to Maldon in recent years: Ring-necked Duck and Green-winged Teal. Both are the new world 'versions' of closely related common species here — Tufted Duck and Common Teal — and this may help explain why they looked very comfortable during their short stays with us.

Ring-necked Duck, Chigborough Lakes, Apr 2013 (SP)

Anything is possible

A great example of how even the most unexpected can turn up is the Eleonora's Falcon that flew over Russell Neave's garden in September 2008. Eleonora's Falcon is essentially a Mediterranean and North African species with only five previous accepted records in the UK. It was probably the last thing on Russ's mind when, while tidying the garden, he saw a large falcon heading towards him. It looked odd so fortunately he wasted no time in taking some photographs as it gained height above him, appearing to feed on insects. These photos helped clinch what would otherwise have been a difficult identification to confirm.

Eleonora's Falcon have a unique lifestyle and are rare (the total world population in 1999 was estimated to be around 6,000 individuals). Their breeding range is restricted mainly to the Mediterranean where they nest on sea cliffs, waiting till the autumn to breed so they can feed their chicks on passing migrant birds. The falcons themselves generally then migrate to winter in Madagascar. It seems, though, that first summer birds, such as the Maldon bird, are somewhat nomadic, ranging widely over Europe, perhaps helping to explain its appearance above Mundon Road!

First summer Eleonora's Falcon, Mundon Road, Sept 2008 (RN)

This was the first live individual to be photographed in the UK

7
MAMMALS

A large proportion of Britain's wild mammal species occur around Maldon, albeit that many of them are not easy to see. There have been major changes to populations over the last century so it is interesting to compare current times with the circumstances described by Henry Laver in his 1898 review of the mammals, reptiles and fishes of Essex. In those days all the squirrels were Red and there were no signs of the likes of Muntjac Deer or Mink. Hunting was then an integral part of country life and game-keeping was having a drastic effect on species perceived as vermin.

Familiar characters

Our current mammals include all the main animal characters from childhood literature and television. As discussed in the paragraphs below, their fortunes have been mixed — their lives have been much less harmonious than often portrayed in fiction!

Rabbit are well established and widespread in the area and can be encountered in all manner of open country and grassland. An easy place to see them is along the eastern edge of the Prom Park, along the track and around the sailing club. During the study period there has been little evidence locally of the myxomatosis that has devastated populations in the past however there has been some impact from the recent arrival of viral haemorrhagic disease that has hit some colonies. The Rabbit's notorious fast-breeding capabilities do help them to recover quickly from losses and currently there are plenty about.

Brown Hare, Hazeleigh, Apr 2018 (SW)

Despite significant declines nationally, Maldon still has a good population of Brown Hare. They can regularly be seen, for example, from the sea wall in the fields South of the Blackwater and in the fields around Lofts Farm and by Scraley Road. They are one of those species that always make your day when seen, ever wary but occasionally affording good views if you remain still. They are most conspicuous when they are courting and they let their excitement get the better of them as they 'hare' about in open fields. Hopefully they can maintain their numbers here in spite of the range of threats they face, including habitat degradation, hare coursing and, more recently, a form of the haemorrhagic disease that appears to be spreading from the Rabbit population.

The outlook for Fox and Badger around Maldon is more promising. Red Fox are amongst the world's most adaptable mammals. Over recent decades, many have learnt to find food and shelter around human habitation, helped no doubt by food handouts from sympathetic residents. As most people no longer keep chickens and rabbits in their gardens, they are now generally looked on benignly and the foxes have lost much of their wariness. In Maldon and Heybridge, these 'town foxes' have become a familiar sight, roaming the streets after dark. Much of their diet is made up of unnatural foods which, judging by the look of some of them, is not always good for their health. Their brazen behaviour and damage to gardens has led to them being branded by some as pests however on balance the public generally seem to find in their favour.

Red Fox, fields south of Maldon, Apr 2015 (JB)

Meanwhile those foxes that follow a more traditional lifestyle in the countryside seem also to be doing well. The activities of the long-established Essex fox hunts have been curtailed somewhat by the 2004 Hunting Act and only a small proportion of the land is given over to poultry farming or pheasant rearing where foxes may come into conflict with their owners.

Maldon's 'country foxes' are every bit as wily as fabled. They have benefitted from the relative health of the Rabbit population but are omnivorous, their diets including everything from fruit to ducklings. At times they can be seen out hunting in broad daylight, travelling some distance in their search for food. A couple of times we have been surprised to see some of our local foxes swimming across the river at high tide from Heybridge to the Prom and from Northey island to the shore, no doubt returning home after paddling over by foot at low tide.

Badger too have proved adaptable and currently have sets all around the district, including large ones at Maldon Wick and Chigborough Lakes. It is likely that they are now more populous in Essex than at any previous time in the last 200 years. Towards the end of the 19th century they were virtually exterminated within the county due to the actions of gamekeepers — it is recorded that around Maldon they had a price on their head. During much of the 20th century they were still being persecuted and their attempts at recovery were impacted by agricultural practices such as the use of pesticides and clearance of hedges. More recently however they have become a protected species and are on the up. The Protection of Badgers Act of 1992 and a generally more sympathetic public have clearly helped — the Badger has now been adopted by the Wildlife Trust movement as a unifying logo. Unfortunately like Fox, they have yet to figure out how to cross roads safely, and most observations are of road casualties.

More carnivores

Weasel and Stoat are also both to be found around Maldon, though their habits mean they are rarely spotted. Weasel are the more frequently encountered, with Heybridge Pits being a regular site. With the narrow cross-section of their bodies, Weasel are ideally designed to hunt voles and mice through the narrow runways they create through rough grassland. As with Barn Owl and Kestrel, their populations must be greatly impacted by loss of hedgerow habitat and the increasing number of domestic cats patrolling the hedgerows that remain.

Historically the Chelmer and Blackwater rivers were a haunt of Otter. A combination of hunting for fur, pest control and sport hit their numbers hard but the final blow to their population was chemical pollution within the river system. One of the good news stories of recent years is that after being granted legal protection and following

the gradual clean-up of rivers, their overall population has now increased and they are once again being recorded locally, having been seen, for example, on the canal and at Heybridge Pits. They remain extremely secretive and have generally been seen only after dark.

Currently the American Mink is much commoner locally than Otter. After escaping or being actively liberated from fur farms, they have successfully colonised much of the UK and have caused considerable damage to native wildlife populations. They have voracious appetites and a highly varied diet that includes birds' eggs, ducklings, amphibians and fish. Around Maldon, they are found along rivers, canals and borrow dykes as well as around Chigborough Lakes and for certain they are having a big impact on our local Water Vole populations.

↑ A rare sighting of local Otters in broad daylight, Chigborough Lakes, May 2021 (JB)

← American Mink, Chigborough Lakes, May 2012 (SW)

Two other mustelids that previously inhabited Essex both became extinct in the late 19th/ early 20th centuries. The last report of a Pine Marten in Essex was in fact from Hazeleigh Wood, in 1884. Polecats, on the other hand, have had something of a resurgence. There has been a steady range expansion, aided in part by reintroductions. The first modern day Essex record was in 1999. They can be hard to distinguish from ferrets (which are essentially a domesticated form of Polecat) but there have been further confirmed records in northern Essex. A very intriguing animal was one that Simon Wood was called in to help rescue near his house in Heybridge in September 2014 — expert opinion was that it was indeed a Polecat and probably a wild one at that.

Smaller mammals

In Laver's day he could write of the (Red) Squirrel that *"it is so well known that very little need be said about it"* and it was considered to occur in all suitable woods, including, presumably, the likes of Hazeleigh Wood. Subsequently the population greatly declined and eventually Red Squirrels became extinct in Essex. By 1960 they were only to be found in east and north-east Essex. Some of the last records, in 1971, were quite close to Maldon, at Woodham Walter and Little Baddow, though it is quite possible that these were just the result of attempted reintroductions as by then the natural population may already have died out.

The squirrels in our neighbourhood are all now Grey. Having been first introduced from North America back in the 19th century, Grey Squirrel spread widely and are now familiar throughout the country. They can be found in all our local parks and woodlands as well as larger gardens, and with no significant predators are often quite brazen in their quest for food, raiding bird feeding stations and regularly finding their way into people's lofts.

In contrast, Hedgehog have been struggling in recent years. The drop in roadside casualties is more of an indication of lower numbers than good news that car drivers and Hedgehog are learning to avoid each other. Challenges for rural Hedgehog include loss of hedgerow habitat, decrease in food availability and increase in Badger, a known predator. Gardens have in the past proved excellent alternative habitat and the Hedgehog's predilection for slugs and other garden pests, as well as of course their general cuteness, make them popular visitors. Use of poisonous slug pellets as well as the trend to enclose gardens with solid fencing have had an impact on Hedgehog mortality and ability to forage. Fortunately, there has been much publicity about making gardens more wildlife friendly so hopefully declines in urban areas can be reversed.

Water Vole are also struggling locally but nevertheless can still be encountered, particularly along the borrow dykes and at Heybridge Pits. As indicated previously, their number one enemy is the Mink. It is to be hoped that continued trapping of the latter will improve their lot. Even more elusive along the borrow dykes is the Water Shrew. Though hyperactive in their pursuit of prey, as with other shrews, their small size allows them to manoeuvre amongst thick vegetation and they remain inconspicuous.

Water Vole, Heybridge Pits, Apr 30 2015 (Stephen Shelley)

Mole are rarely encountered around Maldon as most of the land is either intensively cultivated arable farming or built up for housing with enclosed small gardens. In contrast, Brown Rat do well around the built-up areas — there is a particularly lively population by the quay!

For completeness, mention should be made of the other assorted small ground mammals that can be found locally. Of the mice, the Wood Mouse is the most abundant species, both in the countryside and in and around gardens and houses. Yellow-necked and House Mouse can also occur around habitation, though the latter appears to have very much declined in Essex as agricultural and building practices have changed. The diminutive Harvest Mouse, with its characteristic prehensile tail and ability to construct nests out of tightly woven grass, is an inhabitant of

Wood Mouse (and Garden Snail), Heybridge, July 2020 (SW)

grassland, arable crops and reedbeds. Their numbers are thought to be in decline due to disturbance and loss of habitat but they do still occur in the area, as evidenced by recent records from around Mundon.

Field Vole may be one of the UK's most populous mammal species, however as they favour open areas of long grass, they are rarely seen. The Bank Vole is more forthcoming. They occur in a wider range of habitats and are more likely to be seen in gardens. They seem to have a particular liking for blackberries, and have been sighted feasting in hedgerow bramble bushes.

Our smallest mammalian carnivores, Common and Pygmy Shrew, also frequent the Maldon area. Not often seen, their presence is more often detected by hearing high pitched squeaks coming out of the undergrowth.

All of these small mammals, in particular the mice and voles, form an important source of sustenance for predators higher up in the food chain, including Weasel, Kestrel and all of our owls.

We keep hoping to find evidence of Hazel Dormouse within the study area. However, despite hazelnuts being in plentiful supply, efforts to find them at Hazeleigh Wood and elsewhere have so far been unsuccessful.

Noctule, high above Heybridge, Apr 2016 (SW)

Bats

There is sufficient variety of established woodland, lakes, old buildings and pasture around Maldon for our area to host all of Essex's regular species of bat, ranging from the little pipistrelles that flit around gardens after dark to Noctule that glide high overhead above Chigborough Lakes in the early evening, alongside parties of Swift and House Martin, dining on swarming insects.

Their nocturnal nature makes them challenging to study but the invention of electronic bat detectors and an increase in surveying have led to giant leaps in our knowledge. The sketchiness of historic records has clouded the picture of whether certain species are recent colonists or have been simply overlooked in the past. One of our commonest bats, the Soprano Pipistrelle, was not recognised as widely occurring in the UK till the 1980s — the first recognised Essex record was as recent as 1995.

Two key sites that have been studied in depth by Tim Sapsford and the Essex Bat

Group are Hazeleigh Wood and Chigborough Lakes. All ten of Essex's regular bats have been recorded recently at the former; all but Serotine at the latter. Bat boxes have been put in place at Chigborough and they are being used to monitor breeding and roosting behaviour, particularly of the different pipistrelle species.

Daubenton's Bat hunts by picking prey off the surface of water and can be encountered skimming over the surface of Chigborough Lakes and also the canal, aptly demonstrating why it is also known as 'the water bat'. Meanwhile other bats, such as Natterer's, forage mainly in woodlands. Surveys in recent years have revealed the presence of another woodland bat, the Barbastelle, sound recorded at Hazeleigh Wood. One was caught at Chigborough but was thought just to be passing through, as the habitat there is atypical for them.

The Brown Long-eared Bat is likely found in all habitats locally but tends to be very quiet and so under-recorded in surveys.

Bats recorded around Maldon and Heybridge

Daubenton's Bat
Natterer's Bat
Serotine
Leisler's Bat
Noctule
Common Pipistrelle
Soprano Pipistrelle
Nathusius' Pipistrelle
Barbastelle
Brown Long-eared Bat

Bat monitoring at Chigborough Lakes, Apr, 2018 (JB)

The fieldwork by Tim at Chigborough Lakes has been playing a key part in unlocking the secrets of the Nathusius' Pipistrelle. For some time it has been known to be a migratory species, with populations from Northern Europe moving to the south west for the winter. One of the first proofs of this in a UK context was provided when Tim caught a Nathusius' Pipistrelle at Chigborough in September 2017 that had been ringed in Latvia — the first to be found in Essex! Work is now ongoing to try and confirm the suspicion that the species is also breeding locally.

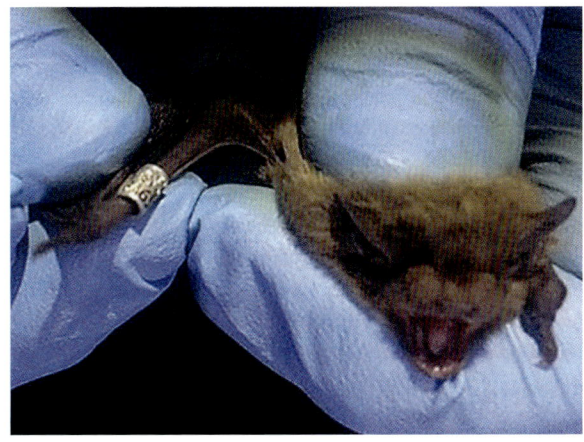

Nathusius' Pipistrelle ringed in Aug 2016 at Riga, in Latvia, and caught at Chigborough Lakes in Sept 2017 (Sarah Sapsford)

Old buildings are often very attractive to bats. Churches, with their high roofs full of dark recesses and access points, are particularly important as roost sites. In the past, a variety of species have been recorded around the old buildings by the river at Beeleigh. One summer, in the early nineties, 1,000 pipistrelles were counted there! There has been a colony of Daubenton's Bats in the mill building (59 were counted emerging on one occasion) and both Brown Long-eared and Natterer's Bats have also been recorded in the area.

Amongst churches, there have been confirmed records of Brown Long-eared Bat at both St Mary the Virgin, near Maldon Quay and St Margaret's at Woodham Mortimer. Full surveys would likely generate records for a wider range of bat species and demonstrate their presence at most of our local churches.

All bats are now protected by law and their breeding sites must be protected but this hasn't been enough to maintain numbers. They need to be able to feed, to roost and to breed. The reduction in cattle farming (many bats eat dung beetles) and general insect populations are a problem. Modern building practice and 'repair' of old buildings have greatly reduced available nesting and roosting sites. Those bats that roost in woodland often use holes and gaps behind bark of old and dead trees. Unfortunately tidying up of many woods removes these features. There is good news at least that bats do often move into artificial bat boxes where they are provided.

It is ironic that it is now, when we are just discovering so much more about them, that their populations are under threat from so many directions.

Deer

The native deer stocks that used to inhabit this part of Essex have long since disappeared, however there are two species that may currently be seen around Maldon. Most often encountered are Reeves' Muntjac. They are a small deer, about the size of a Labrador dog, and native to China. The British population is considered to be descended from escapees from a collection at Woburn Abbey in the early 20th century. They seem to have found our climate and lack of large predators much to their liking and they have spread rapidly. Within Maldon they are becoming increasingly common and have even begun to be seen in gardens within the ring road and in the Prom Park. They have caused problems in some places due to their fondness for shoots and flowering plants, including Bluebell and Primrose, but most people seem to enjoy their presence. Also known as barking deer, their nocturnal calls have become a regular sound within our local woodlands.

Reeve's Muntjac, Langford, Apr 2015 (SW)

The other deer that occurs locally is the much larger Fallow Deer. There is a small herd in the Hazeleigh/ Woodham Mortimer area that have probably all emanated from an aborted attempt that was made to farm deer in the nearby vicinity. They can sometimes be seen early or late in the day in fields in the area and road casualties have occurred on the A414. Two records of Red Deer, by Hazeleigh and Langford, are assumed to have been escapes from farms. Roe Deer could spread here naturally — one seen by Russell by London Road in May 2010 may have been a precursor to more sightings to come.

Sea Mammals

The estuary provides a potential route for all manner of sea life to visit Maldon. In reality the only regularly sighted mammals are Harbour Seal (also known as Common Seal). They follow shoals of fish such as Grey Mullet that move up the river and individuals can stay for some time, such as the one that took up semi-residence between Fullbridge and the Bypass Bridge in Spring 2009 and could often be seen lounging around on the mud opposite the Sunny Sailor. Some of these Harbour Seal have a rusty appearance, due to them hauling out on areas of London Clay, naturally rich in iron oxide.

The North Sea population of Harbour Seal crashed following an outbreak of distemper in 1988. Despite another outbreak in 2002, numbers have now greatly increased — by 2013 they had already recovered beyond their level before the virus took its toll. While they do not breed within the Inner Blackwater, those breeding within the Greater Thames Estuary, from Felixstowe to Deal have been shown to range widely, so hopefully sightings around Maldon will continue to increase.

Harbour Seal, swimming off Maldon Prom, Nov 2020 (JB)

While traditionally scarcer within the region, Grey Seal numbers have also been increasing and they are now regularly seen in the lower reaches of the Blackwater. It was therefore not that surprising, though nevertheless still very gratifying, for John Buchanan and Simon Wood to spot their first within the Maldon patch between Northey and Osea Islands in November 2020, just in time for inclusion in this book!

Sadly local records of cetaceans (whales and dolphins and their ilk) have generally been of remains. The most notable of these was a whale that was found at Maldon back in 1717. This was the first record anywhere of what became known as the Northern Bottle-nosed Whale (in fact the same species that later received media attention when one swam up the River Thames in January 2006). On 23rd September 1900 a young female Minke Whale was driven ashore and killed at the head of Mayland Creek and there is mention of Killer Whale or Orca in 1732 when a contemporary writer "saw two whales which had been killed in one of the creeks of the Blackwater" – exact location unknown.

The most likely cetacean to be seen live within the patch is Harbour Porpoise. Their numbers have recently been increasing around nearby coasts, perhaps due to increases in fish stocks which, in turn, may be due to the fishing-free zones established around new wind turbine installations in the estuary. There have been live sightings as close as St Lawrence Bay but so far the only recent records around Maldon have sadly been of corpses, washed up on the shore, including one found by Russell by the causeway at Northey Island. We live in hope of seeing a live one up this end of the river!

Notably, in November 2014, a pod of 40 Long-finned Pilot whale were reported in the Blackwater off St Lawrence Bay having previously been sighted off Norfolk, Suffolk, Belgium and Kent. After the pod were stopped from stranding at Colne Point by a team from British Divers Marine Life Rescue working with Essex Police, a couple of days later, they re-entered the Blackwater and likely got as far as north of Osea Island if not further towards Maldon. Fortunately the team were able to herd them out to safety and the pod was not seen again, although subsequently an emaciated young female was found dead at Goldhanger.

Part of pod of Pilot Whale in Blackwater Estuary near Osea Island, Nov 2014 (Graham Ekins)

8

REPTILES AND AMPHIBIANS

Barely more than a handful of species of reptile and amphibian are to be found naturally occurring around Maldon, a reflection really of the fact that the UK as a whole is somewhat short-changed in this department. In fact there is no doubt far more diversity amongst the species held by the townsfolk as pets, which could be reasonably assumed to include all manner of pythons, geckos and tropical lizards.

Reptiles

The most frequently seen reptile around Maldon is the Common Lizard. It is found in a range of habitats and on a sunny day can typically be found sunning itself on fence posts. They are readily disturbed however and views are often limited to seeing their tail-end disappearing into the vegetation. The only other lizard we have is the Slow Worm, often mistaken as a small snake due to its lack of legs. With a diet including slugs, worms, snails and spiders they can be found in large gardens and allotments, particularly liking the warmth of compost heaps as sites for breeding and hibernation.

Common Lizard, Chigborough Lakes, Apr 2017 (SW)

Any snake encountered in the Maldon area is most likely to be a Grass Snake. It is a lover of aquatic habitats and a confident swimmer. Chigborough Lakes, the canal and the sea wall borrow dykes are all spots where they might be looked for when the sun is out and they are most active.

The Adder, by contrast, is rare in the area, with only occasional and anecdotal sightings. It is not clear why it is not more common as it is found regularly at other sites in Essex (such as Mersea Island) with similar habitat to some of the sea wall here.

A final, if perhaps unexpected, reptilian group to consider are the terrapins. In the 1990s the Teenage Mutant Ninja Turtles comic characters became cult figures and sparked a fashion for keeping pet terrapins. Unfortunately, they fell out of favour and many terrapins were dumped in the wild by owners who lost interest in them. They have adapted well to life here. There has been a thriving population of Red-eared Terrapins at Chigborough Lakes and Yellow-bellied Terrapins have been seen along the canal and at Heybridge Pits. They have the potential to cause significant harm to the ecosystems that they are in, eating water plants that are needed by other animals and, opportunistically, eating these other animals directly. Thankfully it appears to be too cold for them to reproduce in this country (they are native to the southern United States and Mexico). Those that still remain are likely now to be many years old.

Common Toad, Hazeleigh Wood, Aug 2016
(Maureen Bissell)

Amphibians

In the Maldon area we have just one frog and one toad — the Common Frog and the Common Toad — as well as one common species of newt — the Common (or Smooth) Newt. Although now not so common as their names suggest, they are all still widespread and can be encountered in gardens, particularly those with ponds. They all spend some of their lives out of water but it is the Common Toad that seems most at home on dry land while it seeks out slugs and worms.

There is another newt that occurs in the Maldon area — the Great Crested Newt. It is a lucky animal in that it has attracted a number of special wildlife designations as a European Protected Species, meaning that both it and its habitat has some special legal protection. Essex is a key area for these newts and there is often a risk that new housing developments will impact ponds where they occur. Maldon District Council planning guidelines are in line with the UK Government edicts by specifically requiring developers to review plans regarding risks to Great Crested Newts and carry out any necessary surveys and support mitigation actions.

9
INSECTS AND OTHER INVERTEBRATES

Insects form the largest percentage of the world's known animal species, inhabiting almost every habitat on the planet, so it is not surprising that there are plenty in Maldon! The larger species attract the most attention and here there is huge variety, from nectar loving butterflies to voracious and predatory dragonflies and hornets. They are fascinating to study. While birds and mammals may favour particular landscapes, the needs of insects are often specific to individual plants and there is amazing diversity in their life cycles and behaviour.

Most of our focus has been on butterflies, moths and dragonflies, as reflected in the paragraphs below.

Butterflies

All the common Essex butterflies can be found around Maldon. In total we have recorded thirty two species in the area since 2000. It is the mix of habitats that gives us this good range of species, particularly gardens, woodlands, hedgerows and grassland with wild flowers, though if we had some chalk downs and moorland we might have a few more!

The earliest to be seen are those that have spent the winter hibernating as an adult — Peacock, Small Tortoiseshell, Comma, Brimstone and, increasingly, a few Red Admiral. Peacock and Small Tortoiseshell may be found in garden sheds and, if disturbed or woken prematurely, be seen on a sunny day in January or February. The large yellow Brimstone is often the first to appear out in

Brimstone, Heybridge, May 2020 (SW)

133

the countryside — a signal that spring is beginning. Holly Blue is amongst the earliest to appear in gardens.

Woodlands are good for Speckled Wood and Comma, with Orange-tip and Ringlet along the rides. Hedgerows and grassland attract Gatekeeper, Meadow Brown and three species of Skipper. The sea walls are attractive to the nationally declining Small Heath.

White-letter Hairstreak, Maldon Wick, June 2019 (SW)

While some butterflies are free ranging in their search for nectar and sap, others are much choosier. Hairstreak butterflies have very specific requirements — Purple Hairstreak require Oak trees, while White-letter Hairstreak need Elm. The drastic loss of Elm due to Dutch Elm disease hit the latter hard but small numbers have survived. Maldon Wick EWT Reserve is one place where both these hairstreak species can be seen.

Butterfly interest in summer is augmented by arrival of the migrants — Red Admiral, Painted Lady and Clouded Yellow. Clouded Yellow are particularly attracted to

Clouded Yellow, Wycke Hill Business Park, Aug 2013 (JB)

Lucerne. In recent years this crop has been planted in fields along Limebrook Way and Southey Creek — scanning these on a sunny July or August afternoon can be a good way of spotting these highly active and attractive travellers.

While some species are in decline, such as the previously very common Small Tortoiseshell, others are increasing. The Brown Argus is now regular, helped by it adapting to use a new food plant — Dove's Foot Cranesbill. Marbled White are increasing throughout Essex with several now being seen locally, with the first seen along the sea wall in 2010 and, more recently, inland as well.

A number of woodland species too are spreading nationally. White Admiral is already now established at Hazeleigh Wood but, with increasing sightings elsewhere, we were hopeful that the Silver-washed Fritillary, the largest of the UK's fritillaries

Silver-washed Fritillary, Hazeleigh Wood, July 2019 (SW)

135

Swallowtail, Heybridge Pits, June 2012 (SW)

and a classic species of mature woodland, might colonise too. Sure enough, Russell Neave found a female along Maldon Wick in July 2013 and then, finally, after earlier sightings, Maureen Bissell and Simon Wood observed breeding activity at Hazeleigh Wood in 2019. They were then regularly seen in 2020 and so appear to have successfully colonised.

Even that most celebrated and majestic of woodland butterflies, the Purple Emperor, has now appeared, with one photographed at Hazeleigh by Simon Wood in July 2019.

Thus there is always the chance of something special. One particularly spectacular butterfly was the Swallowtail that was found by Russell at Heybridge Pits in 2012, thought to have been a migrant from the continent. Meanwhile Wall Brown, a species in serious national decline, has been seen twice recently at Lofts Farm, by Malcolm Corbett in 2018 and then by Simon Wood in 2019. And those of us that didn't see it, live in hope that Simon Patient's discovery of a Camberwell Beauty in his central Maldon garden in August 1995 might be repeated!

A full list of butterfly species for the Maldon area is included in Appendix V.

Moths

Moths are an incredible and very diverse group — now considered to even include the butterflies, as a specialised family of day-flying moths. They are a very important group as they are very sensitive indicators of the health of our environment.

Around Maldon we have, on the one hand, hawk-moths as big as the palm of that hand and, on the other, micro moths that you need a magnifying glass to see. Some are flightless, some migrate, some only appear in late autumn and winter and some occur only as females (parthenogenesis – a natural form of asexual reproduction where an embryo develops from an unfertilised egg cell, so a male is not required!). They generally have very specific food plants, after which some are named, such as Oak Hook-tip, Pine Beauty and Maple Pug, although in many cases the moths, or more correctly caterpillars, are actually quite liberal in their tastes and will eat a wide variety of plants.

Eyed Hawk-moth, Hazeleigh Wood, July 2021 (JB)

Cream-spot Tiger, Hazeleigh Wood, Apr 2009 (SW)

There are some moths we really know very little about, particularly some of the smallest ones, the micros, where, for example, their food plant may yet to be identified. Most adult moths are only active after dark so it is fortunate for us that, ironically, a lot of them are attracted to lights. They respond especially to those giving out light at certain frequencies, the best being mercury vapour lights that emit ultra-violet. Both Simon Wood and Russell Neave have been active in uncovering the presence of different moths using light traps in their gardens and, along with Maureen Bissell, at Hazeleigh Wood too. Not all species can be found using lights. Some are known to be attracted to pheromone lures, many of which have recently become commercially available. Experimentation with a range of pheromones during 2020 has given Simon great results, attracting a range of different clearwing species, including the Hornet Moth, a species that uses mimicry to try and avoid predation by looking like, well, a Hornet. Another moth that responds to lures is the impressive Emperor (photo on page 228). Many of the species that respond to pheromone lures are rarely seen day-flyers.

Colourful and rare moths were greatly sought after by Victorian lepidopterists. Many of their favourites have retained the romantic names they gave them. Merveille du Jour, 'wonder of the day' is a moth that still regularly occurs here in woods

Clifden Nonpareil, Hazeleigh Wood, Sep 2019 (JB)

Dewick's Plusia, Heybridge, Aug 2020 (SW)

and parks, the larvae feeding on Oak. Clifden Nonpareil was found at the Clevedon estate in Berkshire and considered 'without compare'. A rarity in recent decades it was an exciting event when Maureen found one in Hazeleigh Wood in September 2019.

Over recent years, habitat and climate-related changes have completely redrawn the distribution map for many species. A big increase in records, and a change in their distribution through the year, suggest that a number of species previously known only as vagrants or migrants, are now breeding locally, including White-point, L-album Wainscot and Tree Lichen Beauty. Another example appears to be Dewick's Plusia, a moth not seen in the UK till one was trapped by Bob Dewick in 1961 at Bradwell-on-

Sea where he had built what was then, and may still be, the world's biggest moth trap. As it had at the time no English name, he was honoured by having his name put to the species. It appeared erratically as a very rare migrant in subsequent years but now sightings have increased to the point where Simon recorded 26 in just a few weeks in autumn 2020 and we strongly suspect they are now breeding nearby. Likewise, Golden Twin-spot, always considered a rare moth in Essex, turned up seven times in Simon's garden between mid-July and the end of September 2020, suggesting that it too is now resident nearby.

This same autumn, in 2020, saw a significant number of some of the most sought after migrants appear. Convolvulus Hawk-moth is a large moth with a long proboscis that can reach down to the nectar in the trumpet-like flower heads of Tobacco Plants. Simon's planting of a row of the latter attracted at least six of them over the period. Going for quality over size is the aptly named Beautiful Marbled, one of which turned up too, just the third Essex record. Perhaps the rarest migrant moth caught during the study period was an Eastern Bordered Straw that came to Russell's trap in Mundon Road in 2003. At the time the first Essex and only the 6th UK record.

Convolvulus Hawk-moth, Heybridge, Oct 2010 (SW)

While the change in distribution of many species is related to climate change, some of the new arrivals here are exploiting our own behaviour and gardening fashions. For example the popularity of planting Leyland Cypress is reflected in colonisation by Cypress Carpet and Cypress Pug. Toadflax Brocade was nationally rare but has become more common as it has taken to feeding on Purple Toadflax, a popular garden plant.

↑ Beautiful Marbled, Heybridge, Aug 2020 (SW)
↗ Eastern Bordered Straw, Mundon Road, Sept 2003 (Graham Ekins)

In all, 919 species of Lepidoptera (butterflies and moths) have so far been identified from amongst those found during the twenty years of our Maldon study. Of these, 4% were butterflies, 46% from the families of larger moths ('macro-moths') and 50% of them from the families of smaller moths ('micro-moths').

The UK's Red Data Book (RDB) lists the rarest and most at-risk resident species. The panel to the right lists Red Data Book species of macro-moths that have been recorded in our Maldon study area 2000–2020.

More statistics on the conservation status of the various moths recorded are provided in Appendix VI.

It must be said that our moth fauna is changing so quickly that review periods for the Red List are going to have to be reduced to keep up with the pace of change!

Endangered:

Oak Lutestring
Golden Plusia
Maple Pug

Vulnerable:

Mouse Moth
Lackey
Sprawler
Pale Brindled Beauty
Mottled Umber
Early Moth
Garden Dart
Pale Eggar
True Lover's Knot
Oak Hook-tip

Dragonflies

Dragonflies are one of the oldest groups of animals on the planet that are still around today. Their ancestors flew through forests during the carboniferous period on two-foot wingspans. Those around in present day Maldon are rather more moderate in size but nevertheless continue to pursue their lives as highly effective aerial predators.

We have an excellent range of species locally of both dragonflies and their smaller siblings the damselflies. The larval stages of all our dragon and damselflies are aquatic and so they depend on water bodies, from the canal, through lakes and pits to dykes and garden ponds. From an Essex perspective there are two particular specialities that we have: the Scarce Chaser, first found along the canal in 2003 and now regular, particularly between Beeleigh and Langford, and the Scarce Emerald Damselfly, more of a coastal species that breeds amongst rushes, often in brackish water, such as found along some of our borrow dykes.

Dragonfly families are generally named after their method of hunting, including hawkers, chasers, skimmers, and darters — their behaviour makes some much more easy to observe than others. The hawkers barely seem to stop moving as they patrol up and down looking for quarry, meanwhile darters continually return to their favoured perches form which they perform sorties when they spot a victim.

Female Scarce Chaser, Beeleigh, June 2008 (SW)

The first adult damselfly to appear each year, generally in late April, is the Large Red, often seen in gardens. Slightly later, the first dragonfly, the Hairy Dragonfly, appears, best looked for near water though it can travel widely and may visit gardens too. Further species emerge as the seasons progress, with June and July being peak months. Towards the end of July, Migrant Hawker make their appearance; whilst some may still

arrive from the continent, they are an increasingly established breeder in southern England and spreading northwards. Migrant Hawker are perhaps the most wide-ranging of our dragonflies, to be seen in many habitats and a regular garden visitor in the autumn. Milder autumns mean that sightings seem to extend later each year. The last dragonflies on the wing are generally Common Darter and Migrant Hawker and they are both regular still in October and increasingly being seen into November.

Dragonflies have had mixed fortunes. Some are struggling. In particular, the Scarce Emerald Damselfly — we are currently only aware of it being found along borrow dykes to the east of Mundon Sluice despite the existence of apparently suitable habitat elsewhere. However others are doing much better, possibly correlated to a

↑ Hairy Dragonfly, South Maldon, May 2018 (JB)

← Willow Emerald Damselfly, Maldon Wick, Aug 2020 (JB)

general improvement in water quality in rivers, canals and other areas of fresh water. Scarce Chaser can now been found along at least three different Essex river systems. Even more dramatically, there has been the arrival into the UK from continental Europe of a number of new species, linked most likely with changes in climate. So far two have colonised Maldon, Small Red-eyed and Willow Emerald Damselflies, and a third, the Southern Migrant Hawker, has begun to appear. A good place to see both the new damselflies is the pond and surrounding vegetation at Maldon Wick EWT Reserve.

More details of these new arrivals are provided in Chapter 13.

A full list of dragon and damselfly species for the Maldon area is included in Appendix VII.

White-legged Damselfly, Beeleigh, May 2016 (SW). A localised and inconspicuous species that can be found along the Chelmer & Blackwater Canal between Beeleigh and Langford

Other Invertebrates

To identify all the other species of invertebrate that occur in the Maldon district would probably take several lifetimes. Invertebrates (essentially, animals without backbones) make up about 97% of all known animal species, with more being discovered every year. The UK has a total of perhaps 35,000–40,000 invertebrates, of which maybe 30% occur locally, a mind-boggling 10,000+ species! The invertebrates comprise many groups of different animals, including insects, arachnids (spiders), molluscs and crustaceans. Each of these groups is split by biologists into different 'orders', which in turn contain different families of similar species.

Our very limited, and what should best be described as casual recording, of orders other than Lepidoptera (butterflies and moths) and Odonata (dragonflies and damselflies) has produced a list of several hundred species around Maldon. What is certainly helping is the publication of new identification books to make it easier to get to grips with some of the groups involved, including caddisflies, bees and hoverflies.

Caddisfly (*Trichoptera*) are closely related to moths but live out their early stages of life under water in cases made out of tiny pieces of grit and vegetation. Such are their attractiveness to fish that they are popularly imitated in the flies tied by fishermen to use as lures. They are a surprisingly poorly studied group but identifications of individuals attracted to moth traps during lockdown have included a species last recorded in Essex during the 1930s, *Grammotaulius nitidus*. Given the numerous bodies of fresh and brackish water throughout the area, the potential for other rarities is high.

One of the biggest insect orders, the Hymenoptera, includes ants, sawflies and wasps. **Wasps** are much maligned but should be seen as the gardener's friend as they consume huge numbers of plant pests annually. Too many people are only too eager to destroy these ecologically important species and then use insecticide in their gardens because they have too many 'pests'! European Hornet have certainly increased locally over the last two decades. These large docile relatives of our commoner wasps can appear threatening but are not unless seriously provoked. A few other wasps have been specifically identified here but many species are very similar to one another and it is a rather specialised area of expertise.

Perhaps best considered to be specialised wasps, **Bees** (*Apoidea*) are obvious and well-known denizens of gardens and countryside, including the Honey Bee and the bumblebees. As well as these social species there are also a large number of solitary

↑ *Grammotaulius nitidus*, Heybridge, Aug 2020 (SW)

A rare species of Caddis Fly (rarer species often have not yet been given an English name)

← European Hornet, South Maldon, May 2005 (SW)

bees, inhabiting (and pollinating) a wide range of habitats.

One scarce bumblebee we have been able to find along the sea wall on the south side of the estuary is Brown-Banded Carder Bee. Remarkably, Simon Wood also found an example in his Heybridge garden, during Covid lockdown.

As with other invertebrate families, new species are now arriving from the continent with astonishing regularity. Tree Bumblebee first appeared in the UK in 2001 and is already now a common resident throughout southern England and locally (photo on page 238). Likewise, the Ivy Mining Bee. First noted in the UK in

Brown-banded Carder Bee, Heybridge, May 2020 (SW)

2001 (it was discovered new to science as recently as 1993), it appears late in the year to utilise Ivy blossom that does not start to appear until September. Simon Wood found a colony at Heybridge Pits in 2016 and they have been spreading ever since.

The most recent bee discovery is the Bryony Mining Bee, which until recently had a south coast distribution, and reached the local area in 2019 when several were found feeding on White Bryony along the canal. Many bees are very small and inconspicuous, and although some have the classic yellow and black markings typical of wasps, many are tiny and black. Amongst these smaller bees, nomad bees are among the most widespread although some of the species are rather scarce. Intensive recording during the 2020 Covid lockdown allowed Simon to record a number of different nomad bees as well as Green-eyed Flower Bee and Wool Carder Bee, giving just a hint of the further discoveries that may await!

Ivy Mining Bee, Heybridge, Sept 2020 (SW)

Grasshopper and Crickets (*Orthoptera*) can be very conspicuous, particularly in late summer when their grating 'stridulations' can be heard coming from longer grass and scrub. Three formally rare species became more common during the study

Southern Oak Bush Cricket, Heybridge, Aug 2020 (SW)

period: both Long- and Short-winged Coneheads and Roesel's Bush-cricket (photo on page 238). Southern Oak Bush-cricket was first recorded in the UK in 2001, the first local records have come in the last couple of years. Intriguingly, it has no real wings, so must have hitched its way here on cars, lorries, boats and trains. Whilst it is thought that the House Cricket, which have been recorded periodically around Maldon in the last few years, are no more than escapees from captivity (they are common live food for reptiles), there must be a possibility that those in Europe may now be heading north, the species having colonised Europe from North Africa.

Beetles (*Coleoptera*) form the largest of the different orders of insects. Most are inconspicuous and unlikely to be seen but they include one of the best loved of invertebrates families — the ladybirds. Typically they are brightly coloured: oranges, yellows and reds contrasting with bold black markings. A lot of the brightest ones are very common around Maldon and include the invasive Harlequin. which was initially feared to be a real threat to our native species but so far, at least, the impact has been less than feared. Of the 'conspicuous' ladybirds recorded locally, the Adonis is probably the one seen the least often. There are also ladybirds that are very small and black, the so called 'inconspicuous' ladybirds, and locally we seem to do quite well for these. The nationally very local Round-keeled Ryhzobius, False Spotted Ladybird and Red-flanked Symnus have all been noted in recent years, whilst in 2020 a *Rhyzbius forestieri* was found in Heybridge, an Australian species first discovered in the UK in 2014!

Although a Stag Beetle, our largest beetle, was recorded in Hazeleigh Wood in the 1990s, there have been none spotted since. Two reasonably sized beetles that can

Adonis Ladybird, Heybridge, June 2020 (SW). A smaller species than our familiar 7-Spot Ladybird

be found throughout the local area are Lesser Stag Beetle and Minotaur Beetle, the latter preferring drier spots. Almost as big as the Stag is the nationally scarce Great Silver Water Beetle, a lover of brackish waters and irregularly attracted to moth traps locally. In all around 70–100 species of beetle have been identified locally.

Great Silver Water Beetle, Hazeleigh Wood, May 2019 (JB)

The Diptera (meaning 'two wing") or **True Flies** are another vast family that is, on the whole, under-recorded, although there are exceptions. For example, the **Hoverflies** (*Syrphidae*) are a more obvious group that include the common Marmalade Hoverfly, which can reach almost plague proportions when huge numbers emigrate from the continent. One of the largest hoverflies is another of those species that is becoming more common around Maldon and Heybridge — *Volucella zonaria* — patterned like a hornet to avoid predation.

Volucella zonaria, Maldon Wick, Aug 2020 (JB)

Spiders have also exploited all corners of our patch. It is often their hunting methods that bring them to our attention. The archetypical webs are probably the impressive spiral webs, spun by the Garden Spider. Not all webs are created for trapping though. The Nursery Web Spider makes a silk sheet to cover the eggs and youngsters like a tent. Another garden species, the Zebra Spider, a small jumping spider, leaps to catch its prey. Flower Crab Spiders have learnt to secrete themselves amongst the florets of buddleia flowers to grasp unsuspecting insects lured by the plant's nectar.

Some species of spider have become particularly well known due to their habit of entering houses. They become most obvious in the autumn, as the outdoor weather turns damp and cold and they look for somewhere warm and dry for mating. Familiar species include the Giant House Spider *Tegenaria gigantea* and the Daddy Long-legs Spider *Pholcus phalangioides*, a species of cellar spider.

Perhaps our most striking spider is the yellow and black-banded Wasp Spider, another recent colonist. Although first recorded in the UK back in the 1920s, its spread has accelerated in the last few decades into Essex — we started finding it locally in 2009. The females are appreciably larger than the males, with a body about 15mm long. They spin a large web incorporating a characteristic zig-zag element (the 'stabilimentum'), often sited across narrow gaps amongst long grass and sedges, with grasshoppers one of the target prey items.

Another colonist to mention, that has received some notoriety in the popular press, is the False Widow Spider. Numbers have increased and it has taken to living in nooks and crannies within our houses — behind cupboards and washing machines for instance. They do give a nasty bite but fortunately are not an aggressive species.

This has been a whistle-stop tour of our local invertebrate fauna — there is still a great deal to learn about this huge and diverse group.

↑ Flower Crab Spider, South Maldon, July 2020 (JB). This one was watched climbing up into the flower head of a buddleia where it waited till a Honey Bee landed

← Wasp Spider, Dump Pool, Aug 2009 (JB)

10
PLANT LIFE

Without any avid botanists amongst our study team, our coverage of flora within the area was not as thorough as we would have liked, however we nevertheless have been impressed by the variety to be encountered. It's hard to explain why, when the colours of flowers have no utilitarian value to us humans, they give us so much pleasure. Perhaps we have an innate recognition of their importance to keeping our world in balance. Furthermore it is the growth and change in appearance of plants that are for many of us the most obvious indication of the passing seasons.

As everywhere these days, the flora around Maldon and Heybridge is a complete mix of native species, deliberate plantings and species that have spread from farm and garden. Plants cannot be caged! Many of the commonest flowers in the countryside are escapees — those that have spread within our area include species from all corners of the world, such as Red Valerian (Mediterranean), Evening Primrose and Goat's Rue (North America) and Opium Poppy (Southeast Europe/ Western Asia). Some of these newcomers cause problems, such as the Spanish Bluebell that is gradually hybridising with/ taking over from our native variety. Others are benign, such as Salsify— originally from the Mediterranean but grown here as a vegetable, and now an attractive addition to the flowers along the sea wall.

Salsify, Southey Creek, July 2013 (JB)

Flowering plants

While we may have no extensive wildflower meadows, we do have plenty of other habitats, each with their own distinctive flora. Throughout the growing months of the year, any walk will be brightened by the flowers that are in bloom. The saltmarsh

↑ Yellow Archangel, Hazeleigh Wood, Apr 2009 (JB). A classic plant of ancient woodlands

↓ Spear Thistle, Southey Creek, July 2009 (JB). Wild flowers are vital for insects (here Six-spot Burnet Moth)

comes alive with Sea Lavender. Along the canal there are the bright yellows of Flag Iris and the complementary hues of Purple Loosestrife. In woodland, Bluebell and Foxglove. Water Crowfoot in the borrow dykes.

The long attraction of these colours is reflected by the names we have chosen for artists' shades — poppy, primrose, cornflower, violet, buttercup...

And as well as the sights, there are the smells — Honeysuckle, Garlic Mustard, Water Mint...

Of course the reason for the colours and smells is to attract pollinators and good numbers of flowers are essential to maintaining healthy populations of bees and other insects.

As gardeners know, the success of plants owes a lot to the nature of the soil they are growing in. Many of our wild plant species thrive in relatively poor soils. Over time our wild environment is becoming increasingly nitrogen enriched from agricultural fertilisers and air pollution. These conditions have resulted in substantial increases in nitrogen-loving species such as Nettle, Bramble, Cleavers, Hogweed and Cow Parsley, to the detriment of species such as Early Dog Violet and Marsh Marigold and to overall diversity.

Some plants need a bit of searching for. Scarlet Pimpernel is not rare but perhaps overlooked due to its small size. It can be found amongst the Common Field Speedwell at the edges of arable fields. The delicate Moschatel, with flowers facing in four directions like a town hall clock, can be found along Mundon Wick and in Hazeleigh Wood. Golden Samphire is regionally scarce but can be found on Northey Island and along the sea wall by Southey Creek. Viper's Bugloss, used in the past as an antidote for snake bites, has been found near to Heybridge Pits.

↑ Scarlet Pimpernel, South Maldon, July 2014 (JB)

← Golden Samphire, Southey Creek, Aug 2020 (JB)

Roadside verges have in the past been an underrated habitat for wild flowers. As highlighted by the organisation Plantlife, 700 species of wild flower grow along the UK's road verges, nearly 45% of our total flora! There are some wide verges beside many of the roads around Maldon, such as the bypass where there is enough room for Gorse to grow.

The maintenance of our verges is the responsibility of Essex Highways. The timing of any cutting is crucial to the ability for wildflower species to grow and survive. Along some roads, such as Limebrook Way, a mixed approach has been used to good effect whereby the verge immediately against the road is cut while that behind is left alone, allowing the different grasses and other plants to grow unhindered. This can lead to some impressive displays of wildflowers, some no doubt the result of deliberate sowing in the past while others being self-sown. The pollinating insects that benefit will not complain however they came to be there! Flowers to be seen along well-maintained verges during the spring and summer include the relatively inconspicuous violets, the familiar and gaudy Dandelion, the subtler yellow Cowslip and then the obvious and showy Oxeye Daisy.

Bee Orchid, Heybridge Pits, June 2017 (SW)

Perhaps the most sought after flowers are orchids. Around Maldon, the two most likely to be found are Bee Orchid and Pyramidal Orchid. As is their wont, their appearances are erratic, but most recently we have found both along the sea wall around Heybridge Pits. Other orchids to look out for locally include Common Spotted Orchid and Early Purple Orchid. Unfortunately the predominance of clay soils around Maldon means we miss out on the orchid diversity to be found in the chalk areas to the south of the county.

Notable trees

As previously alluded to, there is little remaining woodland around Maldon, much of the timber having been felled to satisfy wartime demands in previous centuries. Nevertheless there are a number of trees that demand attention through their age and magisterial appearance. Most notable are the Mundon Oaks, to the back of St Mary's Church. The entrance to the churchyard is itself overseen by impressive Holm Oak and Yew.

There are some interesting trees in the Prom Park. The main entrance drive is along an avenue of Horse Chestnut planted in 1935 in memory of those from the Maldon area who were killed in the First World War. There are Lime lining the upper path and a mix of other kinds of tree, both native and introduced, including oaks, pines as well as some exotics such as a Eucalyptus and a Tree of Heaven. The grandest tree in the park is the Monterey Cypress at the top of the slope at the Western end of the Marine Lake.

↑ The Horse Chestnut Trees in the Prom Park in May 2020, promising a bumper crop of conkers later in the Autumn (JB)

→ A veteran Pedunculate Oak, Chigborough Lakes, Nov 2020 (JB)

Giant Redwood behind The Bell at Purleigh, Nov 2020 (JB)

There are also some impressive old trees in the grounds of the Museum of Power at Langford, including Beech, Sycamore and various cypresses.

There is very little in the way of commercial tree-planting, though some stands of poplars have been established in farmland adjacent to Maldon Wick.

Probably the tallest tree in the area is a Giant Redwood in the churchyard at Purleigh, measured as having a height of 26.1 metres in 2019. There were two Giant Redwood in contention in the churchyard but the other one had its top section blasted out by a lightning bolt in August 2003. There is, though, a neighbouring Cedar of Lebanon that is giving chase.

The Essex Wildlife Trust Biological Records Centre holds data on all reported veteran and notable trees. At the time of writing, besides the Mundon Oaks they note the presence of a large Pedunculate Oak and a Black Poplar at Chigborough Lakes EWT Reserve, a White Willow by the bridge at Langford and a Sessile Oak at the entrance to Great Beeleigh Farm on Old London Road (there is a photo of this last one on page 206).

11
INTRODUCTIONS AND ESCAPEES

The majority of species discussed in the previous chapters made it to Maldon under their own steam. However, there are others that are here only as a direct result of human interventions, including some of our commonest species. Some have been intentionally introduced into the wild, some have escaped from collections, some have hitched a ride. Both Brown Hare and Rabbit were originally brought to Britain to be bred for food, by the Romans and Normans respectively. Both have adapted so well to life in our countryside that it is hard to imagine that they are not native animals. Unfortunately many introductions have had a negative impact on other species. Rabbit have damaged crops and natural habitats through over grazing. Grey Squirrel have out-competed the native Red Squirrel and now cause significant damage to woodlands by stripping the bark off hardwoods such as Oak and Beech.

Domesticated birds gone feral

For millennia, people have kept and bred birds as a source of food. They all began as wild species and then, following generations of selective breeding, have been transformed into a wide variety of different forms, a number of which have since happily spread beyond their farmyard confines and occur commonly in our countryside.

Take the Rock Dove, domesticated for the table and later bred for display and for sport and now to be found around Maldon in a number of guises. The most common of these is the humble town pigeon, known as Feral Pigeon, to be seen around the High Street and adept at eking out a living in the centre of town. They breed in a range of locations including the old warehouses and grain stores around Fullbridge. Then we have the pure white ornamental Fantail Pigeon, kept in dovecotes, and enhancing, for example, the grounds of Beeleigh Abbey. And then in direct contrast, that supreme avian athlete the Racing Pigeon, bred both for its powerful flight and its homing skills, hanging around rooftops close to their breeders' lofts. When competing they can be seen in flocks, heading in fast, direct flight, set on a single compass point. Occasionally, tired, disoriented racing pigeons are encountered on the ground. They can be readily recognised from their sleek appearance and the bling of the multiple rings on their legs. You just have to hope that they can recover before their tameness becomes their undoing and they fall prey to predators.

A whole variety of different forms of Mallard ducks and Greylag geese can also be found locally. These include pure white individuals and birds much bulkier than their wild counterparts. The Greylag are all feral and resident and certainly make their presence known, breeding around the edges of the fishing lakes, hanging out around Heybridge Pits and the river and flying to and fro over the town in noisy flocks. Old farmyard breeds of Mallard live amongst wild birds and much interbreeding occurs. For a couple of years a jumbo-sized drake could be found at the Marine Lake in the Prom Park and tended to dominate proceedings there.

A selection of different forms of duck from within the patch, all derived from Mallard (JB)

Other familiar farmed birds can be encountered around Maldon, including Chicken, Muscovy Duck and Guinea Fowl. In November and December, Black Turkey can be seen out in the open as they are given the chance to be free range for a few weeks before meeting their preordained fate at Christmas — their loud gobbling can be heard for some distance. Recently, one or two farmers have taken to looking after Rhea, large flightless birds originally from South America. There have even been Emu — at the end of our study period, one named Doris was still living at Gardeners Farm along the Goldhanger Road.

Game birds

Game shooting is a long-established pastime around Maldon. To support this pursuit, hundreds or more Common Pheasant are released locally each year along with lesser numbers of partridges (mainly Red-Legged). Since first being introduced to Britain as long ago as Roman times, Pheasant have become widely naturalised. Early introductions were of the

Rhea, Slough House Farm, Nov 2018 (JB)

Caucasian form. Subsequently a wide variety of other races and cross-breeds have been introduced, including Chinese 'ring-necked' races, with their distinctive white collars. Pheasant around Maldon currently range from pure white individuals to very dark *tenebrosus* types.

A 'Blue-back' variant of Pheasant, Langford, Mar 2015 (SW). This form was released in large numbers towards the end of our study period.

Before being let loose, Pheasant are kept in release pens in woodland managed for the purpose. While other wildlife also benefits from this woodland and other game cover it is debatable whether shooting practices are good for conservation overall. There are concerns over the sheer numbers of birds being released as well as the degree to which predator species may be being controlled.

The Red-legged Partridge is also not native to the UK but regularly released for game shoots. Its natural distribution is within the Iberian Peninsula and France however a population was established in the 18th century in Norfolk and they have spread as wild birds. The great majority of partridges around Maldon are Red-legged. Sadly the native Grey Partridge is very much in decline. At the beginning of the study period, occasional Greys were still being seen, particularly by the sea wall by Southey Creek. Now however, recent birds seen are likely to have been released game birds.

Ornamental wildfowl

Another group of naturalised birds were originally introduced by wealthy landowners to enhance their country estates. Canada Geese first appeared in the 17th century and have since spread throughout England, Wales and parts of Scotland. Around Maldon they often associate with the feral Greylags and breed in similar numbers. Each year there are a few mixed pairs of Canada and Greylag Goose, giving rise to some odd-looking hybrid young. In early autumn, further flocks of Canada Geese are to be found on the estuary. It is not clear where they hail from — it may be a dispersal of birds that gathered at Abberton Reservoir for their annual moult.

Egyptian Goose family, Heybridge Pits, Apr 2017 (SW)

A more recent coloniser is the Egyptian Goose. Having been initially introduced to estates in Norfolk, it spread throughout East Anglia and first bred in Essex in 1979 in the Lea Valley. The first local breeding was at Chigborough Lakes in 1998. During the period covered by this book, more have bred at Chigborough as well as at Heybridge Pits. Odd prospecting pairs have been spotted at sites throughout the area, including at Beeleigh, South House Farm and by the Mundon Oaks.

Three other species of introduced wildfowl, Mandarin Duck, Barnacle Goose and Black Swan, all now breed elsewhere in Essex and have been spotted around Maldon too, including a family party of Black Swans in 2009.

A somewhat different story surrounds the Ruddy Duck. Ruddy Duck spread over much of Britain after some escaped from the Wildfowl and Wetlands Trust Slimbridge Centre in the 1950s and early '60s. These bred successfully and the population expanded.

In 1983 breeding began at Chigborough Lakes and they also bred at Hebridge Pits since 1999 or so. However it became apparent that some of this new UK population were travelling to Southern Europe in the winter (in their native America they are migratory). These travellers were then reported to be mixing and pairing with the native and, at the time, increasingly rare White-headed Duck, particularly in Spain. To prevent the risk of Ruddy Ducks causing the demise of the White-headed Duck as a distinct species, our government conceded to requests from other EU governments and mandated that the UK Ruddy Duck population should be culled. In Essex the cull began at Hanningfield and Abberton Reservoirs in 2004. The Ruddy Duck has now been all but eliminated within the UK and have not been seen around Maldon for many years. This is seen as a shame by many as Ruddy Duck are birds with a perky character and smart plumage and were nice to see.

Cinnamon Teal, Heybridge Pits, Nov 2018 (Paul Chamberlain). Probably escapes but who knows?

Various other ducks have also jumped the fence to appear on our local waters. They hail from all corners of the planet — Cinnamon Teal and Rosybill from North and South America, Hottentot Teal from Africa, Bar-headed Goose from Asia and Black Swan from Australia.

Escaped pets

All manner of exotic birds and other animals are kept as pets. We can generally only guess at what may be lurking within local households but occasionally they make their presence known and at times, succeed in making a break for freedom. Perhaps the noisiest local cage bird is the Blue and Yellow Macaw that has lived for many years in an aviary at the back of Daisy Meadow Car Park at Heybridge. The parrot family is a frequent source of escapees — Cockatiel and Budgerigar are good examples that have both been seen at large around our area.

The most successful of these jailbirds has been the Ring-necked Parakeet. A native of the Indian Subcontinent, it turns out that they can survive very well in our climate and thousands now breed in the South East of England, in London, Kent and Surrey. In fact populations have established themselves in many European Cities, including

Ring-necked Parakeet mobbing a Sparrowhawk, Heybridge, May 2013 (SW) — a bit foolhardy perhaps?

Amsterdam, Brussels, Paris, Cologne, Valencia and Rome. They are now slowly colonising Essex. One was seen around Maldon Rugby Club in 2005 and in 2011 a pair appeared around the Hythe, nesting in a tree in Fitch's Crescent the following year. However they were not seen latterly, perhaps being too much of a target for Maldon's Sparrowhawk.

Birds of prey also go AWOL. While being flown by their owners they sometimes opt to stay at large rather than returning to the lure. One popular and easily recognised species that we have seen locally is Harris Hawk. The habit of falconers to interbreed different species, means the identity of some of the escaped falcons we see is a mystery.

As well as unintended escapees there are also times when pets are deliberately released into the wild, perhaps due to the owners finding that their care becomes too demanding or else simply because they lose interest in them. These releases can cause significant damage to other wildlife. In Chapter 9, mention was made of the terrapins that now appear to be established in the area. Other unwelcome introductions are predatory fish, such as a Catfish let loose in the pond at Maldon Wick.

Alien invaders

The species just mentioned in the previous paragraphs were brought to Maldon intentionally. Others have arrived by accident and in some cases have already had or could have a disastrous impact on our indigenous fauna and flora. Even the biggest are not immune from attack. Our English Elm were decimated from the 1920s and then almost wiped out in the 1970s, by different strains of Dutch Elm Disease, spread by the invasive Elm Bark Beetle. During the period covered by this book, two more major attacks on our trees have begun.

Horse Chestnut are now under attack from Horse Chestnut Leaf Miner — the caterpillars of a particular moth, first recorded in the UK in 2002. Leaves are eaten from the inside out and turn brown causing a risk to the health of the whole tree. Although the moths are naturally occurring in Southern Europe it is thought they were brought here on imported saplings. It would be a huge shame if the magnificent Horse Chestnuts that line the entrance road into the Prom Park should come a cropper.

And now Ash Dieback is threatening our native Ash trees. It is caused by a fungus which arrived in East Anglia in 2012, probably also on account of sapling imports.

The Woodland Trust have been predicting that 95% of all UK Ash Trees could perish as a consequence.

Two invasive plants have caused major problems in recent years within our area — Japanese Knotweed and Floating Pennywort. Japanese Knotweed was introduced to Britain in Victorian times but has since spread widely and its fast growth rate and perniciousness are such that it can cause structural damage to houses, as the shoots force their way through weak points in masonry and foundations. A survey in 2019 identified Maldon as one of the hotspots for the species within Essex.

Floating Pennywort, an aquatic plant originating in North America and imported for ornamental use, causes trouble in our inland waterways. It grows rapidly to form a dense mass across the surface of the water, suffocating other life within it. First found at large in Essex in 1991, it is now a big problem along our section of the Chelmer and Blackwater Navigation and persists despite great efforts from the Chelmer Canal Trust and others to control it.

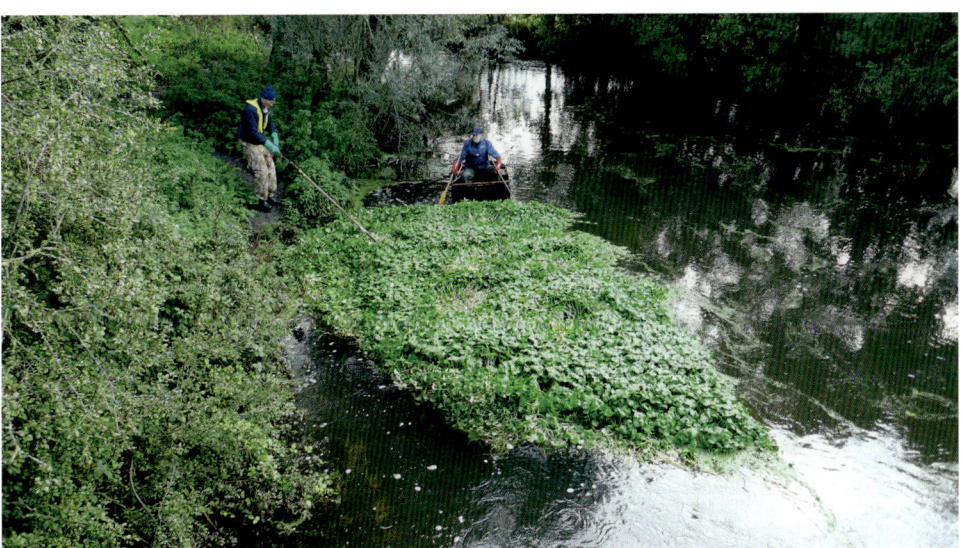

Clearance of invasive Floating Pennywort from the canal, Oct 2020 (Chelmer Canal Trust)

Himalayan Balsam is another invasive plant that has caused problems nationally. Locally it is currently not that prevalent, though it can be found in the Millennium Wood, between the leisure centre and the recycling centre.

Various invasive insect species have also recently appeared amongst us. One of the most attractive is the Harlequin Ladybird, it was introduced into Europe from Asia to try and control aphids. It found its way into the UK around 2003/4 and has presented a threat to native species of ladybird, by out-competing them for food and eating their eggs and larvae. They can now be found throughout Maldon and Heybridge in gardens and even indoors. The Box-tree Moth is an even more recent arrival as an alien import. It is indigenous to Asia but has spread throughout Europe, first appearing in the UK in Kent 2007 and now to be found throughout South East England and beyond, with large numbers appearing around Maldon and Heybridge in 2020. As the name suggests, its larval food plant is Box — the caterpillars have the capacity to completely defoliate box hedges, so becoming the absolute nemesis of topiarists.

↑ Box-tree Moth, Mariners Way, Oct 2019 (JB). By 2020 people were reporting large numbers throughout Maldon and Heybridge

→ Manila Clam, Southey Creek, Dec 2020 (JB). Introduced to the Blackwater in the 1990s for the restaurant trade, now spread widely along the estuary. Gulls have learnt to open them by dropping them onto the sea wall

12
CHANGING POPULATIONS

The times they are a-changing

A common theme throughout this book has been change and in many ways the period we have been discussing has seen it reach an unprecedented level.

Several of the contributors have known the Maldon area for well over 30 years. In that time, large new estates have been built to the south of Maldon and in all directions around Heybridge. All this has dramatically changed the environment. This new housing has not been bad for all wildlife — the bird population density of wildlife friendly gardens can be higher than intensively managed farmland. The casualty has been overall diversity.

The key for particular species is if, and how quickly, they can adapt to change. Over time, many have been able to adjust their diets, utilise new nesting sites or take advantage of a reduction in predators. Back at the start of the 20th century, William Glegg was describing both Magpie and Goldfinch as 'somewhat uncommon residents'. Both are now common even within the built up areas of our town. The pigeon family seems particularly adaptable. As well as Feral Pigeon and Collared Dove, Woodpigeon too have been moving into populated areas. In recent years Stock Dove are also beginning to be seen in Maldon's gardens. Collared Dove benefitted from the surge in satellite dishes during the 1990s and subsequent decade, finding the bracket and space between dish and wall ideally suited for their nests, though the switch to cable television and internet is bringing an end to this niche.

The principal drivers to change amongst the wildlife populations of Maldon are:

- Increased human activity (including habitat loss through increased housing)
- Agricultural intensification
- Climate change

People impacts

The dominating presence in the area is that of our own human population. Such is our nature that almost all of our actions impact the neighbourhood around us, as we are building and extending our homes, driving around in our automobiles or simply partying in the park.

How to characterise our habits in the period 2000–2020? When outdoors we have been busy doing a myriad of different things: gardening, promenading, football playing, dog walking, parkrunning, skateboarding, fishing, birdwatching, cycling, gig rowing, kite flying, picture taking, crabbing, pigeon shooting, Pokémon tracking, picnicking, orienteering, sunbathing, sailing, Morris dancing, wildfowling, geocaching, barbecuing...

Some of these are clearly of no real worry to our wildlife but unfortunately there is not enough space for all. One dog a day having a swim in a pond may not be a problem but if it happens on an hourly basis then it probably is. The disturbance caused by, for example, jet skis doing turns along Southey Creek is unsustainable. When microlights are flown up the river, the pilots may marvel at the site of large flocks of waders flying up from their roosts, but these birds have been trying to get some much needed rest over the high tide — this unnecessary disturbance is most unwelcome.

↑ Remote control yachts on the Prom Park boating lake. No impact to wildlife
↗ Jet Skiers along Southey Creek. Disturbance to all birds roosting along the creek

In the last few years, drones have arrived on the scene. No longer the preserve of dedicated hobbyists, they are now available to a mass market and are being seen increasingly flying around our airspace. Hopefully licensing and bylaws can be put in place to prevent excessive and irresponsible use.

On the positive side, recent years have seen a greatly increasing general interest in wildlife. Membership of the Royal Society of the Protection of Birds has reached 1.2 million and that of the Essex Wildlife Trust, over 39,000. The popularity of television programs such as BBC's Springwatch can only be positive news for the prospects of the animals featured in them.

Mention should also be made of what has become one of the area's other most numerous mammals. The increase in our human population has brought with it a parallel increase in the pet population of Maldon. The People's Dispensary for Sick Animals (PDSA) 2020 report estimated that while more people own dogs, the total UK cat population still outnumbers that of dogs. Going by their national averages, as the human population of Maldon and Heybridge is now well over 20,000, there are at least 4,000 pet cats in our area. Despite being fed by their owners, many of them will spend a lot of time out and about, following their instincts, staking out bird tables or hunting along field hedgerows for small mammals that in the natural order of events would have been prey for Barn Owl, Kestrel, Weasel and Stoat.

Agricultural intensification

With the need to feed increasingly demanding consumers whilst trying to remain financially solvent, there is relentless pressure on farmers to make their businesses more efficient. Sadly for wildlife, many actions taken with the best of intentions have a negative impact on biodiversity.

- Larger fields with fewer hedges remove valuable niche habitat
- Extensive use of pesticides and herbicides and use of washed seed create monocultures with no wild flowers and minimal insect life
- Intensive sowing regimes with two crops/ year and autumn ploughing meaning no winter stubble and spilt grain for wintering birds to feed on

As well as food, farmland birds need nesting sites. Hedgerows are valuable but ground nesters need suitable areas too. All too often, fields are worked right up to the edge — leaving uncut margins helps not only birds but also a multitude of small mammals and invertebrates.

The significance of farming methods is highlighted by the dramatic changes that can unfold when farmers have implemented wildlife friendly initiatives. At Iltney Farm, east of Mundon Sluice, when a stretch of land beside the sea wall was set aside and left to grow wild for a while, there was a clear increase in wintering larks, finches and buntings. These in turn attracted birds of prey, including Merlin and the nationally scarce Hen Harrier.

The affordability of environmental actions is greatly influenced by the farming subsidies that are available. For many years the 'set aside' incentive encouraged farmers to take land out of production, however this scheme was phased out in 2008 due to a push by the EU to increase cereal supply. In the meantime, the Environmental Stewardship scheme has been supporting certain specific actions, such as improvements to water quality and work to help farmland wildlife.

With Brexit, the whole system will change as the EU Basic Payment System phases out. At the time of writing, the UK government is starting to unveil what it says will be a radical new approach, named Environmental Land Management, to drive general improvements to the farmed environment. Of course it remains to be seen to what extent it delivers on its aims.

In a separate initiative to improve the management of land for nature, advice for landowners is being provided by the Campaign for the Farmed Environment, a partnership of agricultural, environmental and governmental bodies. They have produced a set of guidelines with the aim of "promoting good environmental management through productive farming practices".

There are some good examples locally where actions have been taken by landowners that have resulted in better habitat for wildlife. One is the creation of a new fishing lake and associated tree planting in the farmland just north of the layby on the A414 on the way into Maldon. Another is the establishment of a plantation at Mundon Wash, with mixed native trees and managed hedgerows that are already providing nest sites for a range of species.

New fishing lake established just north of the main road into Maldon

Climate related changes

Our long term prevailing temperature and weather has regularly fluctuated. What is concerning now is that the current general temperature rise, exacerbated by human activity, is happening at an unprecedented rate and faster than nature can evolve and adapt to. Many natural processes, from germination to hibernation, are triggered by warmth and cold. Different elements of an ecosystem can get out of sync. An oft-cited example is that of the timing of Blue and Great Tit broods. Traditionally, hatching has been timed to coincide with availability of Winter Moth, Green Oak Tortrix and other caterpillars. However, the caterpillars are now appearing earlier, meaning they have peaked before the tits need to feed their chicks. There is evidence that tits are adapting to bring forward their egg laying but they are still out of step.

The British Trust for Ornithology coordinates a range of population surveys and they have picked up on a number of birds whose populations are on the move. Colder climate species such as Meadow Pipit and Willow Warbler are shifting north — declines of both these species have been noted around Maldon over the past twenty years and we believe Meadow Pipit, at least, may now be lost as a breeding species here. The Willow Warbler is being replaced by increasing numbers of Chiffchaff. There is sadly no such equivalent species to fill the void being left by Meadow Pipit.

House Martin populations are also decreasing locally — this may also be a drift of the population to the north but it is likely also to be due to reductions in nesting sites and insects to feed on.

As we are finding, current climate change is not just about gradual warming but also increases in extreme weather events. After hot spells, including a record breaking heat-wave in 2006, it did seem that cold winters might be a thing of the past. However any snowman building residents of Maldon were given ample opportunity in the winter of 2009/10. The harsh weather was hard for the birds, though there were some rewarding sightings for birdwatchers, including a Smew on the river off the Prom, three Great Northern Diver off Osea Road and an influx of Woodcock.

Another kind of weather extreme was experienced in August 2013, when a period of

Maldon
Prom Park
under snow,
Jan 2010

167

↑ Flooded fields, South House Farm, Aug 2013
← Cormorant, Beeleigh, Mar 2018 (JB).
A casualty of the 'Beast from the East'

heavy rain caused significant flooding. The fields at South House Farm turned into mini-lakes attracting lots of waders including a flock of seven Ruff — normally we only see singles of this species.

The wildlife impact of weather is related to timing. In February 2018, the country was savaged by a particularly harsh wave of cold weather: the 'Beast from the East'. It brought a fortnight of unusually low temperatures and heavy snowfall. Fieldfare seemed to appear in every garden, desperate for food as the ground they normally foraged on had frozen.

The BTO Breeding Birds Survey of the following season showed that there had been big losses amongst smaller birds — Goldcrest, Long-tailed Tit and Wren. Nationally Kingfisher declined by 38% year on year and it is likely that the losses in Moorhen were also due to the 'Beast'. Locally, Barn Owl were particularly badly hit, with numbers still to fully recover. To make matters worse, later in 2018 there was a period of significant drought which also impacted prey populations.

Two years later, we experienced a new extreme — in August 2020 we had three successive 'tropical nights', when the temperature remained above 20° C from dusk to dawn. All told, it has been two decades of unusually erratic weather: hot and cold, wet and dry, interspersed with good blows as the after effects of North American hurricane seasons have breezed across to us.

Lost or on the way out

The consequence of all the issues discussed in the previous paragraphs has been that during the 20th century, the UK breeding bird populations of a great many species fell catastrophically. Sadly, though not surprisingly, this has been reflected in some species being lost entirely from the Maldon area. Two examples of species lost from Essex that were once widely distributed are Red-backed Shrike and Willow Tit. The former was lost as a regular UK breeding species in 1989, while the latter has the unfortunate honour of being described by the Rare Birds Breeding Panel in their 2018 report as being the UK's fastest declining species. There were still 4–5 pairs of Red-backed Shrike around Maldon in 1948, but just single pairs in each year until its last stand here in 1954. The last record of breeding Willow Tit around Maldon was slightly earlier, in 1943.

Until the early 1990s, Tree Sparrow could still be seen in their hundreds during the winter, for instance, there was a flock of up to 200 at Heybridge Pits in February and March 1983, but a rapid decline ensued such that, apart from a couple of isolated records, none have been seen locally in the last twenty years. They were breeding just outside the patch at Ulting in the 1970s/ 80s and quite likely also bred inside the

Spotted Flycatcher, Beeleigh Abbey, June 2016 (SW). The last known record in breeding season

patch in that same period. They are now extinct as an Essex breeding bird — the last breeding record in the whole county was in 1999.

In 2000, at the start of our study period, we had seventeen UK Red-listed bird species breeding in our area. However by 2020 we appear to have already lost at least one of these, Spotted Flycatcher, with others at risk of being lost in the next few years. Spotted Flycatcher, a charismatic migrant, was quite common until about fifteen years ago but they have now stopped nesting at the last known local site at Beeleigh Abbey. Some are still seen passing through Maldon on migration but even these numbers are reducing, reflecting the species' national decline. Latest data from the State of the UK's Birds 2020 report, published by the RSPB and others, suggests that the UK population declined by 88% between 1970 and 2018.

There are sadly nine further UK Red-listed breeding species that are at risk locally. Of these, the most concerning are Turtle Dove and Lesser Spotted Woodpecker as both have UK populations that are in general collapse. Between 1970 and 2018, the UK population of Turtle Dove fell by 98%; between 1970 and 2015, that of Lesser Spotted Woodpecker fell by 83%.

Only twenty years ago, Turtle Dove was a common breeding species in the area with, for example, nine pairs at Chigborough alone in 1996, whilst a migrating flock of 144 was at Heybridge Pits as recently as August 1993. Now they are reduced to odd pairs with occasional sightings of migrants and it is to be feared that we will lose them as a breeding bird locally within the next 2–3 years. Continued illegal hunting in the Mediterranean is compounding an already critical situation for the species.

There were occasional sightings of Lesser Spotted Woodpecker in various locations over the period however the only breeding season records have been from Hazeleigh Wood and even these have become sporadic. It is likely that recent records to the south of Maldon are wandering individuals from remaining sites around Little Baddow and Danbury.

Willow Warbler, Chigborough Lakes, May 2016 (JB)

Nightingale are also disappearing nationally at an alarming rate. Like Turtle Dove they too are migrants and face multiple challenges on their journeys each year. They appear to be maintaining their numbers at their main local stronghold at Hazeleigh Wood but numbers elsewhere are erratic. In recent years Maldon Wick and the canal towpath by Langford have perhaps offered the best chances of hearing them from a public footpath.

While not Red-listed from a national perspective, it looks as though Willow Warbler are now barely hanging on as a local breeding species, with Chigborough Lakes the last recorded location. The great majority of birds heard singing each spring will be just migrants passing through on their way north.

As already mentioned, traditional farmland birds are also in dire straits. Grey Partridge probably only survives now, to the south of the town, due to introductions by game syndicates. Yellowhammer are now distinctly uncommon, with isolated breeding pairs around the fringes of the study area. Corn Bunting too have declined but we are lucky in this area in that we do at least have reasonable numbers in winter when flocks of several dozen can be found along Southey Creek and by Mundon Sluice, and also in smaller numbers at Heybridge Pits. In the spring, they disperse from the Maldon area onto the Dengie peninsula to breed with only a few pairs staying to breed locally, with a concentration around the fields and hedgerows in the general area of Mundon.

Yellow Wagtail, Mundon, May 2015 (SW)

Yellow Wagtail have suffered not only in their wintering grounds but through loss of suitable wet pasture to breed in. Although they remain relatively common on passage, breeding appears to be now confined to the limits of our patch at Lawling Creek and possibly in farmland to the north of Lofts Farm and Chigborough. Trends in the status of Hobby are more difficult to assess. Despite long term national increases, linked to warmer climate and increasing dragonfly numbers, reduced sightings over the last decade point to a decline locally.

A decade ago, the saltmarsh along the Blackwater hosted regular breeding pairs of Meadow Pipit, Redshank, and Oystercatcher. As previously mentioned, Meadow Pipit now seems to have gone as a breeder (though many still come to winter each year). Redshank appears to be going the same way, with pairs now breeding only at Lawling Creek — they are probably struggling to find suitable nest sites as most of the saltmarsh up to the sea wall is now regularly covered by high tides. There were just two pairs of Lapwing still breeding in the patch in 2020, again at Lawling Creek, down from eleven in 2005. Unlike the previously mentioned saltmarsh birds, which are all ground-nesting species, Oystercatcher frequently nest on raised positions, such as on banks and even on man-made structures such as mooring posts. This affords them more protection from peak tides and they are still breeding successfully around the patch.

There is more information on Maldon's UK Red-listed bird species in Appendix II.

Other forms of wildlife have also been suffering. Regular surveys organised by Butterfly Conservation have highlighted many declines. Locally, the elm-feeding White-letter Hairstreak is perhaps now confined to just a couple of sites, although they can be notoriously difficult to find. Whilst moth diversity has remained similar over the last few decades, what is undeniable is the reduction in overall numbers – witnessed by fewer "splats"

Garden Tiger, Mundon Road, July 2005 (JB). A colourful moth in serious decline

on the car windscreen. Butterfly Conservation have reported that during the 40 year period from 1968 to 2007, the total abundance of larger moths across the southern half of Britain reduced by 40%. Some species, once common, have almost disappeared locally, the most impressive-looking of these being the Garden Tiger. Another loss has been the Glow-worm. Previously they were regularly found along the old railway line at Maldon Wick but sadly they have now gone, perhaps due to warmer summers meaning fewer of the snails that their larvae feed on or due to the embankment becoming too overgrown.

Cetti's Warbler, Heybridge Pits, Mar 2016 (SW). An elusive species — much more often heard than seen.

Increases and newcomers

It is certainly not all bad news though.

While it is disheartening to contemplate the species that are disappearing, there are newcomers appearing on the positive side of the balance sheet that can add some cheer to our lives. A time travelling naturalist from the early 20th century would be amazed to see some of the birds that are now amongst our most conspicuous species: the Little Egret feeding along the river, the Avocet at the edge of the mud and the Collared Dove that are now amongst the commonest of garden birds. And while the Robin may still be our number one year-round songster, the recently arrived Cetti's Warbler beats it in decibels.

Wildlife has always sought to exploit new opportunities. Changes in the environment have worked in favour of some species historic requirements, while others have been able to adapt their diet or behaviour to gain an advantage.

The Collared Dove is a species that has really cracked it. At the start of the 20th century, its population was generally restricted to Asia, with a small foothold in European Turkey and the Balkans. It then spread remarkably, reaching Czechoslovakia in the 30s and the Netherlands and Denmark in the 40s. The first UK records were in the 50s. In the subsequent half century they have widened their range throughout the British Isles.

The Cattle Egret is another global champion. From a base in Southern Iberia and tropical Africa and Asia it started spreading to Southern Africa and Central America in the late 19th century. By the mid-20th century it had reached the United States, Canada, Brazil and even Australia, its success being ascribed to its feeding habits enabling it to spread to wherever there are herds of cattle to follow.

Cattle Egret, Limbourne Creek, June 2020 (JB)

Meanwhile it has also been spreading through Europe, breeding for the first time in the UK in 2008 and now, as mentioned in an earlier chapter, breeding successfully locally at Chigborough Lakes since 2019.

It has been fascinating to find that the period 2000–2020 that we are focusing on in this book has coincided with an unprecedented wave of avian colonists into the Maldon area. These include natural arrivals from the continent (Egrets, Cormorant, Avocet, Cetti's Warbler), species changing their habits (Herring and Lesser Black-backed Gull, Common Pochard and Gadwall) and introduced species (Egyptian Goose). Just why all these should arrive within a space of just 20 years is a question worthy of future study when current trends can be compared with future states.

All the species involved and the details of their arrival are listed in Appendix II.

Great White Egret, off Maldon Prom, Sept 2018 (JB)

As well as those that are already now established here, there are other birds that we are seeing increasingly in the summer and which may be on the brink of settling too. Bearded Tit may now have bred in a couple of sites, at the reedbeds east of the Osea Causeway and at Heybridge Pits, and there has been some breeding activity seen from Marsh Harrier as well. For several years, pioneering Mediterranean Gull have been spending the summer amongst the Black-headed Gull at Heybridge Pits and surely it won't be long before they start breeding too.

There have also been increasing sightings of Great White Egret and it is likely they will soon start breeding elsewhere in Essex. However as they generally nest in extensive reedbeds, there is probably insufficient habitat for them around Maldon. At the other end of the size scale, the diminutive Firecrest, jointly holding with Goldcrest the title of the UK's smallest bird, is also being encountered more frequently. On more than one occasion, males have now been encountered singing here in the spring.

Perhaps even more remarkable, and certainly unanticipated by most, has been the arrival of colonising insects. For years, the number of dragon and damselflies to be seen in the UK comprised a fixed number of traditional breeding species and a handful of rare migrant visitors. Then one by one, species arrived that general naturalists had not even heard of! The first UK record of Small Red-eyed Damselfly was at Bradwell-on-Sea in Essex in 1999, and it has since spread as far as Devon and North Yorkshire. It has been breeding locally for some time: one readily accessible site has been the pond at Maldon Wick. The next species to make an appearance was the Willow Emerald Damselfly. The third UK record was only in 2007 and yet by 2013 we were seeing them at Beeleigh Falls. They can now be found all around the patch, breeding at the Prom Park, Heybridge Pits and Lofts Farm amongst other places.

The latest to reach us has been the Southern Migrant Hawker, also known as the Blue-eyed Hawker. The first Essex records were in 2010. There were more records in subsequent years and then in 2020 they started appearing all over the county, including individuals locally at Limbourne Creek and along the borrow dyke by Mundon Sluice.

As explained in Chapter 10, there are newcomers from many of the other groups of invertebrates too, including butterflies, moths, crickets and bees. Amongst the bees, the Tree Bumblebee has spread widely and is commonly to be seen in local gardens and the Ivy Mining Bee is now another to look out for. After Simon Wood first finding a colony in 2016 at Heybridge Pits they have now been seen in other sites where there is plenty of Ivy. Other species being seen more often around our homes and gardens are European Hornet and False Widow Spider. Fortunately neither of these are the dangerous monsters they have been depicted as in some of the popular national press!

Amongst long established species there have been some increases as well. At the start of our study period, Coal Tit were virtually unknown away from Heybridge Wood and the Langford/ Beeleigh area but they have now spread and are regularly breeding in Hazeleigh and Kent Woods to the south of the patch, with occasional birds now also being seen in gardens within Maldon and Heybridge themselves.

↑ Southern Migrant Hawker, Limbourne Creek, Aug 2020 (JB)

← Marbled White, Southey Creek, June 2018 (JB). Sightings of this attractive butterfly are on the increase

For no obvious reason, Nuthatch were absent from our local woods at the start of this century, despite being regular in woods around nearby Danbury. Since 2015 they have started to be seen around Hazeleigh and now in Mundon Furze and Kent Wood too, breeding in the latter.

Blackcap seem to be more than holding their own, being found in most wooded areas and often singing from ornamental trees in and around our housing estates. Jackdaw are also being seen more often and, as previously eluded to, they are beginning to move into potential breeding sites around the town. The clouds of Jackdaw coming to winter roosts can be very noisy — they seem to share with Black-headed Gull and Greylag Geese a blatant disregard for attempts by humans to find peace and quiet outdoors! The Black-headed Gull colony at Heybridge Pits has grown to the point where birds nest on virtually every spare patch of ground on the islands and spits, with 5–600 pairs counted in 2016.

Estuary birds

Given Maldon's important natural role as a wintering site for wildfowl and waders, it is good to note that there have been increases amongst several of the key species. Birds move around the estuary, so it is probably best to consider numbers for the Blackwater Estuary as a whole. Every month, teams of observers carry out counts of wildfowl and waders all around our coast as part of the British Trust for Ornithology's Wetland Bird Survey (WeBS). Their dedication (often in the face of challenging weather) produces data that can be used to understand population trends.

Flock of Dunlin over the estuary, Mar 2016 (SW)

The following paragraphs look at changes over recent years in Blackwater Estuary WeBS counts and national WeBS counts as well as international trends. (The International trends are from the reports published by the secretariat of the UN-sponsored Agreement on the Conservation of African-Eurasian Migratory Waterbirds).

For the key species for which the estuary is most important internationally, the changes over the ten years up to the winter of 2018/2019 are shown in this table:

Changes in winter populations of key species over 10 years

	Blackwater Estuary	Whole UK	International status
Brent Goose (Dark-bellied)	+26%	+5%	Stable
Black-tailed Godwit (Icelandic)	+55%	+31%	Increasing
Dunlin	+44%	no change	Stable
Grey Plover	-2%	-20%	Decreasing

Data compares 5 year averages of peak WeBS counts
– average of 2014-2019 compared to average of 2004–2009

In three of these cases the Blackwater population has increased. For Black-tailed Godwit this correlates with an increase and expansion of the breeding population and range in Iceland. With the Brent Goose and Dunlin, the local numbers have increased while the international status has been stable, meaning the extra local birds are probably due to a change of distribution, possibly due to habitat degradation or climate change elsewhere.

Of the twenty most numerous species of wildfowl and wader on the Blackwater, there are seven that have declined over the last ten years: Wigeon, Mallard, Lapwing, Ringed Plover, Grey Plover, Golden Plover and Curlew. Most of these are considered to be decreasing internationally as well and are therefore a clear cause for concern.

It is worth noting that with all but two of these twenty species, the overall UK population has performed worse over the last ten years than the Blackwater one, meaning that, in relative terms, the Blackwater Estuary has become increasingly important as a wintering site.

Our own experience has shown that some of the species that occur in much smaller numbers, Goldeneye, Green and Common Sandpiper and Common Snipe, are also showing signs of local decline. This may be due to changes in wintering location but perhaps is more likely due to gradual thinning out of their overall populations.

One of the species that has significantly increased around the estuary in winter is Avocet, reflecting increases in their breeding populations on both sides of the North Sea and English Channel. They are one of a number of species that are being seen increasingly at the Maldon end of the estuary, others being Dunlin, Knot, Bar-tailed Godwit and Pintail. All can now be regularly seen from the sea wall at the south-eastern end of Heybridge Pits and often off Maldon Prom too. It would be nice to think that this change in distribution is as a result of the actions taken over the past few years to improve the water quality of the river and canal. ***More data on these estuary bird populations is included in Appendix III.***

Returnees

Perhaps more so than the newcomers, it has been enjoyable to welcome returnees, species that were lost from Maldon in the past but have since come back. A key message is that if conditions have not been completely wrecked, nature has an ability to recover. In many cases all it has taken is for people to stop poisoning or persecuting them! This is particularly true of raptors.

The prime examples are Sparrowhawk and Common Buzzard. Sparrowhawk numbers crashed in the middle of the 20th century, a key factor proving to be organochlorine pesticides such as DDT that they ingested from their prey, which in turn caused their eggshells to become critically thin. By the 1960s only a handful of Sparrowhawk nested in the whole county. Following banning of these pesticides numbers began to recover. Now they can be considered one of our regular Maldon garden birds.

Previously abundant, Common Buzzard populations were continually persecuted during the late 18th and the 19th century to the point of extinction as a breeding bird over much of Britain. The last Essex nest found was at Purleigh in 1865, the eggs being taken by a collector.

↖ Sparrowhawk, Maldon, Apr 2020 (JB). Recovered from near extinction in Essex to become common and widespread

← Common Buzzard chick, Hazeleigh Wood, June 2014 (RN)

Apart from an isolated record in the 1950s, Common Buzzard began summering again in Essex in the 1980s and breeding in the 1990s. At the start of this century, summering Common Buzzard could be watched from Lofts Farm, soaring over the woodland to the north. They have since increased greatly to the point where they can be regularly encountered along the A414 and other main roads. In 2014 a pair bred at Hazeleigh Wood and there are now isolated pairs around Mundon and also at the extreme north of the patch. In 2020 they probably also bred at Lofts Farm. A survey in 2020 by Adrian Dally in the West Dengie/ Mundon area suggested that Common Buzzard were now challenging the Kestrel as the area's commonest raptor.

Like Sparrowhawk, Peregrine were also affected by DDT and hit a UK low in the 1960s, though occasional Peregrines could still to be found in winter, as chronicled in J. A. Baker's contemporary accounts of them hunting along the Chelmer Valley and Blackwater Estuary. Peregrine populations are now on the increase and have been boosted by their adapting to nesting on tall buildings and other man-made structures as alternatives to the natural cliffs they have traditionally used. Whilst they have not started nesting within Maldon or Heybridge, they do now nest on the power station at Bradwell and the 'Jumbo' water tower at Colchester. Hunting birds are now being seen in all months of the year around Maldon (though predominantly still in the winter).

Two other avian predators are also making a comeback: Red Kite and Raven, one with human assistance, the other on its own accord. During the 20th century, Red Kites became virtually extinct in the UK, with just a remnant population left in the old oak woods of mid-Wales. With protection and feeding programmes, the Welsh population began to recover. From 1989 the Nature Conservancy Council and the RSPB began a reintroduction in the Chilterns that proved highly successful, using birds translocated from Spain and have been followed by further reintroductions elsewhere in the UK. The progeny of the reintroductions have now spread widely, probably helped by their wandering habits in their first year before they settle down to breed. The first contemporary Maldon record was at

Red Kite, Heybridge, Aug 2020 (SW)

Langford in 2002. Since then records have increased dramatically. The first confirmed modern nesting in Essex was in 2016. There are now multiple local records each year of birds passing through — surely it will not be long before they start to breed here?

With reduced levels of persecution, Raven, like Common Buzzard, have been able to spread out from strongholds in wooded hillsides to recolonise Eastern England. They began breeding again in Essex in 2014, near Hatfield Forest, and now breed in other parts of the county too. The first modern local record was one flying out of Hazeleigh Wood in November 2019 and with another over Heybridge Pits in December 2020 there will surely be more to come!

Mammalian predators are also returning. A survey conducted in 1986 produced no sightings of Otter anywhere in Essex. Subsequent surveys have demonstrated a gradual return to many of the river systems, including those of the Stour and the Colne as well as our own. As mentioned in Chapter 8, Otter are now being seen again within our Maldon patch. They will certainly have a positive effect on the ecosystem if they help drive out Maldon's population of Mink. However their fondness for fish brings them into conflict with fishing interests and there are reports of Otter being killed. Otter are such marvellous creatures that let us hope the fishermen can live and let live.

Now that Polecat and, since 2019, Pine Marten too, have started to be reintroduced in different parts of England it will be interesting over the coming years to see whether they will also find life around modern-day Maldon to their liking. Polecat are already being increasingly reported in Essex and as mentioned earlier, there has been one recent tantalising record from Heybridge.

Elsewhere in Essex, near Finchingfield, European Beaver have now been reintroduced as part of a rewilding initiative but this is a long term project, not suitable for all river systems, so it is unlikely we will see any near us any time soon.

Reintroductions are also helping the re-establishment of lost butterflies, with both official and unofficial releases taking place of a range of species in potential breeding habitat. In 1984, the Heath Fritillary was introduced to nearby Thrift Wood (by Bicknacre). However, despite dedicated management to support its food plant, Cow Wheat, this colony has now died out.

Silver-washed Fritillary and Purple Emperor are more wide-ranging and it is hoped that reintroductions at the Marks Hall Estate near Colchester may lead to further colonisations elsewhere. Whether recent local records of these last two are due to these reintroductions or butterflies from their currently expanding natural populations may be unknown but either way it is good news to see them flying again in the woodlands that were their home in the past.

13
THE FUTURE

General trends

The fact that there has been so much to write about in the previous chapter is a demonstration of the breadth of challenges facing our local animals and plants. Unfortunately, there is no magic wand that a lone individual can wave to fix everything. Their fate often lies not just in our own hands but also in the actions and cooperation of people elsewhere. The majority of the birds seen around Maldon are migratory species and many depend on breeding and wintering areas in distant lands and, for those that do not make the journey in one hop, secure resting and feeding stations en route. For example, the Knot that winter with us arrive from breeding sites in northern Canada and Greenland via a stopover in Iceland.

Species have evolved to have some tolerance to short term setbacks. The UK population of the Common Whitethroat, one of our commonest warblers, crashed by 77% in 1969 due to a severe drought in their wintering grounds in the Sahel region of Africa.

Knot, off Heybridge Pits, Mar 2021 (SW)

However, they have now recovered to the point where they are common again and widely distributed around Maldon. To give another example, in past decades Song Thrush populations were also declining significantly, perhaps due to issues around pesticide use and the drying out of soils affecting food availability. They appeared doomed but they too seem to be staging a recovery.

One strategy that can help is an ability to have large or multiple broods in a season, to assist recovery when times are good. This greatly assists species that are particularly susceptible to bad weather, such as Barn Owl and Kestrel that struggle to feed in hard winters.

Unfortunately, this natural resilience has its limits and the current pace of environmental degradation has been proving too much for wildlife to withstand. Whilst species losses are to an extent balanced by some new colonists and there are some positives, the underlying trends have been a reduction in biodiversity and a thinning out of general wildlife populations. The situation in Maldon very much mirrors what is happening in the rest of the country.

The 2019 UK State of Nature Report, published by the National Biodiversity Network, confirms the situation — across 696 terrestrial and freshwater species there has been a decline of 13% in average abundance since 1970. With a drop of 6% over the past 10 years alone, clearly this decline is firmly established and ongoing. There have been some species showing population gains, very often those that are more generalist or that have adapted to man-made environments. The remaining paragraphs of this chapter consider the outlook locally regarding the main pressures involved.

Climate trends

Average global temperatures continues to rise. In 2018 The International Panel on Climate Change were saying that just limiting global warming to 1.5°C above pre-industrial levels "would require rapid, far-reaching and unprecedented changes in all aspects of society". If unchecked, the biggest immediate risk to Maldon and Heybridge will be flooding. As temperatures increase, thermal expansion and melting ice caps will cause average sea levels to rise. Combinations of higher tides and extreme weather will be increasingly likely to cause our current sea defences to be overwhelmed.

We had a close scrape on the night of 5/6th Dec 2013 when much of Heybridge was evacuated due to the risk of a tidal surge. Fortunately damage was less for us than further north in East Anglia, where sea walls were breached, as locally the peak of the storm did not coincide with peak tide.

The risks are graphically depicted on UK Government Flood Warning web pages.

Risk of flooding around Maldon and Heybridge

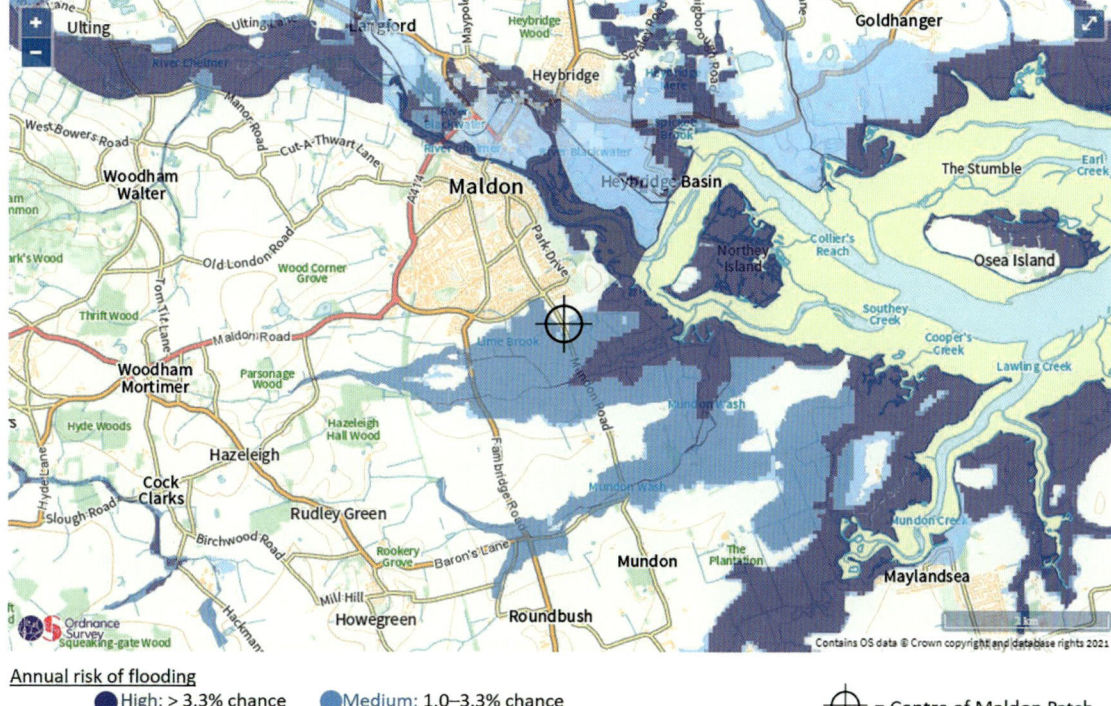

Annual risk of flooding

● High: > 3.3% chance ● Medium: 1.0–3.3% chance
● Low: 0.1–1.0% chance ● Very low: <0.1%

⊕ = Centre of Maldon Patch

Data from UK Government Flood Warning Information Service (retrieved 25 May 2021)

As has been described in the previous chapter, the increase in average temperatures is already changing the distributions of many species. They face multiple challenges. Those of our present species that would try to move to the north may find that suitable habitat is not available. Meanwhile, southern species seeking to move into the UK and spread into Maldon may struggle because their traditional food plants or animal prey may not be available, as different elements of the food chain are adapting and spreading at different rates. These circumstances will always favour the generalist and adaptable species over the specialists. A warmer climate also provides more opportunity for accidentally introduced invasive species that are from regions of warmer, drier climate to colonise.

Throughout time there have been periods of major climatic change. Entire ecosystems have come and gone as a consequence. We need to be wary that if we continue to aggravate the climate, it might be our own ecosystem and *Homo sapiens* that fails to survive this time!

Increase in human population

In recent decades, the United Kingdom's human population has continued to increase at a significant rate — by 4% during the last fifteen years of the 20th century and a further 10% in the first fifteen years of this one. Maldon and Heybridge's new housing developments will help with the demand for additional housing but there will very likely be pressure for further expansion in the future. The extra housing space is being achieved by building on green fields, there being no large expanses of brownfield space that might be used locally. The impact of more people, traffic and need for additional amenities will clearly increase pressures on wildlife. How this plays out will depend greatly on the level of sympathy that people have for the environment and their preparedness to leave space for the animals and plants that need their own space.

Litter pick carried out by Friends of Heybridge Gravel Pits, March 2015 (photo from the group's Facebook site)

It is certainly an interesting time to be considering the future. Three key circumstances are likely to drive substantive changes to the way society behaves. One has been concern about climate change. Initially a driver for adhoc climate protests and strikes, it has now become manifested in formal recognition as an emergency by numerous national and local governments and other parties, declaring that urgent action is needed to reduce climate change to avoid potentially damaging and irreversible changes to the environment. During 2019 a number of local councils in the UK began publishing climate emergency declarations. In February 2021 Maldon District Council joined them, agreeing to adopt a Climate Emergency Statement, with the stated aim of making Maldon District Council carbon neutral by 2030 and encouraging all other agencies in the district to achieve the same.

The second main change driver is the development of a whole range of new 'green' technologies to enable reduction of CO_2 emissions and more sustainable use of materials. Banks of wind turbines off the Essex coast and expanding use of solar panels offer carbon neutral energy supply. By 2020, electric cars have evolved from being mere novelties to proven designs being actively marketed by all the major automotive companies.

A third, and completely unanticipated event, has been the Covid 19 global pandemic that hit the UK in spring 2020. This is one new species that we did not want to see arrive in Maldon! At the time of writing, with the UK still in lockdown but vaccinations in progress, there is hope that some form of normality will begin again soon but it remains to be seen what the long term impacts will be. No doubt the economy will take time to recover, which could mean a lack of funding for actions seen as non-critical. There is a real risk that this could reduce funding for wildlife rangers and conservation work.

Many sought solace during lockdown by spending more time with nature, becoming more aware of it as they explored new routes during their daily exercise walks. Wildlife programming on television was hugely popular and there has been increased public engagement in wildlife observation and photography — on line participation in the RSPB's Big Garden Birdwatch in 2021 was 85% up on 2020.

Hopefully this awakened interest will help shape an environment that will be more supportive of our wildlife going forwards.

Need for protection

Whatever the long term prognosis, there are sufficient short term challenges to mean that for us and our children to enjoy and benefit from the wildlife currently around us we need to protect it now. Many of the species we appreciate most — the birds of prey, the migrant songbirds, the familiar farmland species — are amongst the most vulnerable. One of the most immediate issues is mitigating the impact of the new housing developments currently being built. All developers are required to follow the Maldon District Design Guide. This specifically requires developers to give consideration to existing district biodiversity action plans and "seek to design out or minimise biodiversity impacts at an international, national or local level". Maldon Town and District Councils need to ensure that the developers deliver on these obligations and all planning applications must be diligently reviewed to ensure decisions take full account of the relative environmental impact of different proposals.

If we consider a wider, international perspective, the main wildlife value of the Maldon area is as a passage and wintering ground for wading birds and wildfowl and it is the protection of these that we should prioritise. As explained in the previous chapter, for the key species, the numbers on the Blackwater Estuary over the last ten years have bettered the national trend, meaning that from a UK context, the Blackwater is becoming more important as a refuge for wintering birds. Ways need to be found to protect roosting areas and avoid excessive disturbance to them, which may mean striking a balance between fishing and boating interests and maintaining space for the birds.

With so much of the land around Maldon and Heybridge farmed, how it is managed has a sizeable impact on our local wildlife. There are some big questions that will need addressing as we go forwards, such as whether and how different kinds of pesticides should be licensed and on the use of genetically modified plants. Hopefully decisions will be made that can protect our wildlife as well as ensuring that farming is kept profitable and the nation is fed. Hopefully the system of subsidies to be enshrined within the UK Government's new Environmental Land Management scheme will achieve their desired outcomes.

Currently around Maldon and Heybridge, very little of the land outside of private hands is actively protected. The main wildlife reserve is Chigborough Lakes Essex Wildlife Trust Reserve. The benefits of limited access and reduced disturbance are immediately apparent if the wildlife of this reserve is contrasted with that of adjacent fishing lakes. It is doubtful if the thriving heronry would have flourished in a more public area.

Essex Wildlife Trust's other local reserve, at Maldon Wick, can hopefully maintain its role as a wildlife buffer. Previously it was surrounded by farmland but it will in future be sandwiched between two new housing developments. The only other significant piece of land owned by a conservation organisation is the National Trust's reserve at Northey Island.

The Essex Wildlife Trust's Biological Records Office maintains a list of all local sites that have been recognised as having special wildlife value — Local Wildlife Sites (**see Appendix VIII**). The list is shared with Maldon District Council but the great majority have no special protection in place. In particular, none have been designated as Local Nature Reserves. The largest site crying out for greater protection is Heybridge Gravel Pits. Hopefully arrangements might be made with the landowners to ensure the wildlife value of the pits can at least be maintained or even enhanced.

Many of the most valuable habitats are the old ones. It takes years to establish the type of coppiced woodland most favoured by Nightingale. Oak trees must be mature before they can support their full biodiversity potential.

Nevertheless, seemingly simple actions can make a difference too. Swift nest boxes, bat boxes, garden ponds, wildflower plantings and clearance of invasive plants from our waterways all help.

Gardens managed for wildlife can benefit a wide range of smaller species, such as moths, butterflies and bees, which depend on specific microhabitats to provide the food plants and breeding sites that they require.

To keep our diversity of animal life we need to fully maintain and protect the full diversity of habitats that we currently have in the area.

Bug hotel in South Maldon garden, July 2020 (JB). (Holes used as nest chambers by Red Mason Bee)

Predictions for our local wildlife

So in the face of all these challenges, what if we look into a crystal ball and try and predict what changes to our fauna and flora we might experience over the next few years?

As previously explained, it would sadly be no surprise if we lost some of the breeding birds that have already been in serious decline. This could include Turtle Dove, Lesser Spotted Woodpecker and Willow Warbler. Hopefully, with some continued habitat management, Nightingale and some of the struggling farmland birds may yet be able to hold on.

The nature of the estuary does not look set to change any time soon and with improving water quality looks set to remain a haven for wintering birds, so long as excessive disturbance of high tide roost sites can be avoided.

On the mammal front, the chief risk is perhaps Water Vole. If Mink are not kept in check, and if the borrow dykes are not looked after properly, they will be in trouble. More awareness of the needs of bats and greater protection of existing/ provision of new roosting and breeding sites will surely help them.

But what of the new arrivals and re-colonisations that so much of this book has discussed?

It is likely that some of the species that have just gained a foothold may become more established. This could include a couple of duck species, Common Pochard and Gadwall, as well as the new kid on the block, Cattle Egret.

With the expanse of available factory roofs it is likely that the colony of Herring and Lesser Black-backed Gull will increase further. Although these gulls are seen by some as a nuisance, overall numbers in the UK are declining and Natural England have stated that licenses to control them will only be granted in exceptional circumstances.

The colourful (if raucous-voiced) Egyptian Goose is likely to become widespread — they are already breeding readily and can have large broods.

New avian colonists over the next few years could include some or all of the following:

- Red Kite — several pairs now breed elsewhere in Essex and local sightings are increasing. One of the larger woods, Hazeleigh, Kent or Heybridge Wood must be in the running for the first breeding attempt.
- Red-crested Pochard — several pairs now breed at Hanningfield Reservoir and there have now been sightings around Maldon in all seasons.

Red-crested Pochard, Lofts Farm, Jan 2021 (JB)
Sightings of Red-crested Pochard are increasing so it may well be a species that starts breeding here in the next few years

- Mandarin Duck — slowly increasing elsewhere in Essex and Chigborough Lakes would appear to provide suitable habitat.
- Mediterranean Gull — a pair at Heybridge Pits seems long overdue, given how often they have been seen prospecting the area in recent years.

- Ring-necked Parakeet — already bred once, currently spreading eastwards from Metropolitan Essex.
- Raven — increasing numbers year on year in Essex. A pair bred successfully in the Dengie peninsula in 2020, only five miles from the centre of Maldon.
- Firecrest — records increasing across Essex, with several records now of singing birds around Maldon.

Other species now colonising East Anglia, such as Great White Egret, Spoonbill and Goshawk, are less likely to start breeding here due to a lack of suitably extensive nesting habitat, however we can anticipate an increase in records of roaming individuals...

Looking even further to the future, Osprey, Black-winged Stilt, Penduline Tit, Bluethroat and Serin are all possible colonists, especially if some of our sites are sympathetically managed. Erecting an Osprey nesting platform in the middle of Heybridge Pits may not be a daft idea!

The future should also provide some good mammal sightings. Hopefully Otter will become better established and, if not persecuted, become less secretive and easier to see. Newcomers could include Polecat and Roe Deer. Both are spreading into Essex, with numbers increasing.

First local sighting of a Serin, Heybridge Pits, Nov 2016 (Stephen Shelley)

There are also more insects on their way. There are several migrant dragonfly species that we have been looking out for, including Red-veined Darter and Lesser Emperor. Another dragonfly species, the Norfolk Hawker (otherwise known as Green-eyed Hawker) is also now on the horizon. As the name suggests, they were traditionally found in Norfolk but recently they have been spreading from the continent and are now breeding in Kent. In 2020 there were multiple sightings elsewhere in Essex so hopefully we will see one soon.

Of the damselflies, Southern Emerald, which is now breeding in southern Essex could well arrive here too, in the wake of recently established Willow Emerald.

Lepidopterists are out looking out for a new butterfly: the Southern Small White. Very similar in looks to our regular Small White, it is a continental species that has been rapidly advancing northwards and at the time of writing has already reached Calais. And of moths, amongst those we are expecting soon is the striking Jersey Tiger — they are currently spreading into Essex from London at a fast rate.

Oak Processionary Moth, Heybridge, Aug 2020 (JB)

However with moths there are major concerns as well. The Box-tree Moth has already arrived and begun decimating Maldon and Heybridge's Box hedges. Gypsy Moth, another pest species, is beginning to colonise too (our first local record was in July 2018). Worryingly, we have also started encountering Oak Processionary moths. Spreading from the continent, their caterpillars have the ability to strip the leaves off our oak trees. As was the case with the Elm and Dutch Elm disease, our native Oaks have never previously encountered some of these immigrants from the continent so have not evolved to defend themselves.

With all the changes, both foreseen and unforeseen, that will happen over coming years, let us at least hope that Maldon can still remain a home to the popular favourites, those species that have inspired poets for centuries and become part of our folklore, those such as Nightingale, Cuckoo, Skylark, Tawny Owl, Water Vole and Brown Hare.

It will be interesting to see whether any of the newer arrivals gain similar popular resonance and whether future novelists will include Little Egrets and Muntjac Deer amongst their casts of wildlife characters!

14
THE TEAM, THE STUDY

'The Team'

The core team, for this venture, has comprised John Buchanan, Simon Wood, Russell Neave, Emma Neave-Webb and Simon Patient. We are all enthusiastic naturalists, though for the most part we have been saddled with having to hold down jobs to pay for our beer money rather than being able to spend all of our time in the field. To flesh out the book we have readily incorporated records from a great many other observers from the area. We are very grateful to all of them for sharing their experiences — fuller thanks are in the acknowledgements section at the end of the book.

Provenance of records

Fortunately, we have not had to follow the approach of past times when birds were shot to prove their identity. The use of cameras and quick communications mean that the great majority of the more interesting/ unusual records were readily corroborated. All the rare bird records included in the study have been accepted by the Essex

Cycling round the patch on a bird race, Simon Wood (left) and Russell Neave, Oct 2010 (JB)

Birdwatching Society's identification panel and/or the British Birds Rarities Committee where appropriate.

Details of historic records have been taken from the Essex Birdwatching Society's past annual Essex Bird Reports and/ or the various Essex avifaunas listed in the references section.

The majority of scarcer invertebrates have been photographed and identifications confirmed with relevant county recorders.

What have we missed?

Amongst the more obvious groups of animals that we have focussed on in this book, there are still some that have evaded us!

These omissions include those that breed unobtrusively, or lurk in areas away from those regularly visited. It took quite some time to confirm Water Pipit as a regular wintering bird — as well as looking very similar to the commoner Rock Pipit, one of their traits is that thy spook easily and then immediately fly off into the far distance.

It is possible that Garganey have bred in the past and Firecrest is quite possibly colonising under our noses.

One potentially regular bird that we may be missing entirely is a gull. Over recent years, Caspian Gull, a relative of the Herring Gull from central Europe, has been shown to be wintering regularly in South Eastern England in small numbers. Unfortunately we have yet to nail one locally but it is highly likely that, at times, odd individuals have joined the large evening gull roosts out in the estuary. It is possible that other rarer gulls, such as Iceland and Glaucous Gulls might also roost there on occasion

Distant view of gulls roosting between Northey and Osea Islands, Sept 2018 (JB). There could be all manner of rarer species amongst them!

but as most gulls fly in to roost only as it is getting dark, and as the middle of the river is about a kilometre from the nearest sea wall, observation of the roosting gulls is challenging to say the least!

Other missed species may well be lurking amongst the throngs of waders that gather on the mudflats at low tide and we are still trying to pick out an American Wigeon amongst the hundreds of Eurasian Wigeon that regularly winter.

And of course there are all the birds we have been missing as they have flown by out of sight, either too high or during the hours of darkness. Increasing numbers of people are now running sound recorders overnight to pick up, and afterwards identify, the calls of whatever is passing. With 80% of migrant bird species being nocturnal migrants, investing in and using this equipment would be a great way to increase our understanding of the night-time avian traffic over Maldon and maybe add some more species to our list.

Regarding mammals, it is some of the smaller mammals that have proved most difficult to confirm. Despite some effort in searching, particularly around the stands of Hazel growing in the eponymous Hazeleigh Wood, we are not aware of any proof of Hazel Dormice in any of our local woods.

Saltmarsh Horsefly, Heybridge, Aug 2020 (SW)
This is a UK Red Data Book listed rarity from a group that doesn't get the attention of the more glamorous butterflies and dragonflies

Of course if you turn to less studied groups of animals there is almost limitless opportunity to add to our knowledge of Maldon's natural inhabitants. This might include beetles, spiders, flies, fungi…

The worry is that we may be losing some species before we even knew they were here!

We will end this chapter with a great example of how wildlife can always produce surprises — the story of perhaps one of the most unexpected additions to our patch list in recent years. In December 2019, South Woodham Coastguard Rescue Team received a call that there was a sea turtle by Mundon Creek. Amazingly, the body of a 1.7 metre Leatherback Turtle was by the sea wall!

Leatherbacks are the world's largest turtles and renowned ocean wanderers. The Atlantic population mainly breeds in the Caribbean but they are adapted to survive in cold water and they travel all over in their search for the jellyfish that they like to feed on.

Sadly, by the time it was found, the turtle was already dead, however it was assumed to have been still alive when it swam up the creek. The rescue team were able to recover the body so that it could sent to the Natural History Museum for examination and possible display.

↑ Leatherback Turtle, Mundon Creek, Dec 2019 (South Woodham Coastguard Rescue Team)

→ The rescue team with the Leatherback Turtle, Dec 2019 (South Woodham Coastguard Rescue Team)

15
A MISCELLANY

Maldon Pubs and Beer

It is true to say that the idea of this book, and much of the research required, have been galvanised by planning sessions in Maldon's pubs. Pubs and ale drinking have a long tradition here. Some of the pubs we have frequented do have wildlife links, or have outside tables that have provided some good wildlife watching, which seem reasons enough to discuss them briefly here.

Beer has been brewed in Maldon from at least the Middle-Ages, when the White Canons were based at Beeleigh Abbey. In times since, Maldon has been full of pubs, particularly while the town was booming as a port. Over the course of the study we were lucky to have two award winning breweries within the town, both brewing excellent ale. The **Mighty Oak Brewing Company** was founded in Brentwood but then relocated to West Station Yard in Maldon in 2001, from where it has brewed ever since.

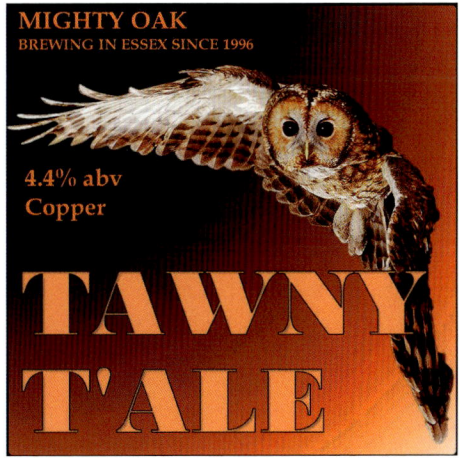

Two bird- themed beers, brewed locally by The Mighty Oak Brewing Company

Farmers Ales began in 2002, setting up within the grounds of the Blue Boar Hotel, later transforming into the **Maldon Brewing Company**. In recent years, the two breweries have each operated micro pubs along the High Street — the **Mighty Oak**

Tap Room and **Farmers Yard** — both very popular and, on occasion, extremely lively. In 2019, 'The Yard' was voted 'Pub of the Year' by the Maldon and Dengie region of the Campaign for Real Ale.

Sadly the ramifications of the Covid lockdown have hit all breweries hard. Whilst Mighty Oak have been able to continue brewing and delivering beer to thirsty souls around the county, the Maldon Brewing Company has been sold. Farmers Yard itself has been retained and is currently being operated as a bottle shop, selling a wide range of beers and ciders as well as some cask ale.

The **Blue Boar Hotel** dates back to the second half of the 14th century. For many centuries it was a coaching inn for those travelling from London. It retains much of its historic charm. Within the public bar there are some old cabinets of hunting trophies and at one point a punt gun was mounted above the fire place. It is easy to imagine it being the place where punt gunners and other wildfowlers used to meet to sup ale and discuss the day's haul in days gone by.

For a while, our pub of choice was the **Carpenters Arms**, to the back of the Blue Boar. It was in a good position in terms of where we were all located at the time and served an excellent range of beers. Bird-themed beers we enjoyed over the years

The Blue Boar Hotel, near the top of the High Street

included Dark Star's "Partridge" and Green Jack's "Waxwing". The strength of the beers did prove a problem at times, both in terms of managing to stagger home and in remembering anything we had agreed to do afterwards.

Along the river there are the **Queen's Head** and the **Sunny Sailor** — both good places from which to watch life pass by. Little Egret and other wading birds can be seen on the mud and we have seen Harbour Seal from both. John's first Maldon Red Kite was seen from the Sunny Sailor — there had been sightings of one all over Maldon that day and his wife Jan made the propitious suggestion that rather than haring around trying to catch up with it we should wait for it to come to us while we drank a beer!

The Queen's Head, on the Hythe

The **Hurdlemakers Arms** in Woodham Mortimer has a large beer garden with old fruit trees (some of the plums were in the past used as an ingredient for Farmers Ale's Spiced Plum beer). A happy memory here was one sunny afternoon spent drinking Mighty Oak Blackbird ale while the real thing was belting out his song from a tree above us.

The **Bell** at the top of the hill at Purleigh affords a great view over the area and is adjacent to the churchyard, with its Giant Redwood and breeding Goldcrest and Coal Tit.

Of course there are other local pubs that one might highlight — the Queen Victoria along Spital Road, the Maltsters Arms, the Jolly Sailor at Heybridge Basin — but to mention so many might suggest that the authors have an over eager enthusiasm for ale! Perhaps the best location for views was the Mill Beach Pub, though sadly it is currently closed. As well as being a great place to look out over the estuary, it was also a venue for live music and, in recent years, Wassail and a number of other traditional festivals were celebrated there.

Patch Watching as a Sport

One idea spawned in the pub was that of seeing how many birds we could see in 24 hours within our patch. The target we set ourselves would be to find a hundred different species.

Our first attempt was in January 2008 and a team total of 102 species was achieved, beginning with a hooting Tawny Owl and ending up with 4 Little Egrets spotted at their roost at dusk (if they had not been white we would not have picked them out!).

We repeated the exercise in subsequent years and found it a great way of comparing populations year to year and at different times of the year.

Motivated by the cycling exploits of others elsewhere in Essex, in 2010 we decided to attempt a non-motorised Maldon patch day list, choosing that year's May bank holiday to try to capture the incoming summer migrants alongside lingering wildfowl and waders, as well as some passage birds. The team comprised John Buchanan, Simon Wood, Russell Neave and Simon Patient. Emma Neave-Webb joined us for the final couple of hours.

In case it is of interest to anyone trying this in the future, the day played out as follows:

Maldon Bird Race 7th May 2010

Half the fun of this kind of event is in the planning. The route was agreed over a pint at the Swan at Little Totham: we would begin with an early start to catch the dawn chorus at Chigborough, then on to Osea and round the sea wall back to Heybridge, up to Langford and back, and ending with a final stretch along the southern sea wall to Mundon Sluice.

After a night of heavy showers we gathered at 4am at Maldon Wick in pretty much complete darkness (since 2009 the council had been switching off the street lighting overnight). The silence was just beginning to be broken by Robin, Blackbird and the odd call from Mallard, Moorhen and Pheasant. Checking we were all together, we then headed off around the bypass. A Fox barked in the distance and then a Skylark began singing — with absolute clarity in the still, cool air. As our convoy headed into Heybridge we failed to spot the broken fragments of a bottle on the road and Simon Patient's tyre was wrecked. Fortunately he had a spare bike at home so he wheeled his disabled bike back to South Maldon while we continued on to Scraley Road.

At Chigborough we were met by a mixed chorus from the heronry, with a backing of Tufted Duck, and struck lucky with our first Nightingale and some very vocal Tawny Owl. As we walked round the lakes a Garden Warbler was in song (unusual here) and at 4.45 it was just getting light enough to see it. As we crossed over to Lofts Farm, it was getting slightly warmer but it began to rain. A Kingfisher sped over the water, a Barn Owl flew over and the regular Black-necked Grebe favoured us with an appearance. In amongst the rain showers a party of hirundines appeared over the water, including both Sand and House Martin in amongst the Swallow.

By now Simon Patient had caught up with us again and we conducted one more lap of Chigborough before looping round to Osea Road. With relief we found there were still Brent Geese and some waders around. Our raptor list increased by a Marsh Harrier and some distant Common Buzzard, while a couple of Wheatear were a welcome boost. In desperation to increase the list further, I then made the day's biggest gaff, by initially calling a distant assemblage of flying Egrets and Crows as Feral Pigeons! Eventually we did succeed in finding a real Feral Pigeon.

The cycle round the sea wall from Osea to Heybridge was very enjoyable and we enjoyed a well-earned cuppa and bacon butty at the Heybridge Cafe at around 11 o'clock, already on 81 species. We were surprised at the numbers of Bar-tailed Godwit about and there were plenty of Whimbrel and Greenshank but sadly no sign of the recent Spotted Redshank or, on Heybridge Pits, the sub-adult Little Gull or Mediterranean Gull. Simon Patient then picked up a distant Hobby and a brown bird flying low towards us over the water had us briefly confused — not a wader but a rufous-phase Cuckoo!

A singing Meadow Pipit and a late Common Teal were useful additions as we left the Pits and began the long cycle up the canal to Beeleigh. However the pace had slowed. Willow Warbler and Mistle Thrush helped and then, at last, species number 100 — a Coal Tit, in an area of trees which we were searching for Treecreeper. We never did manage the latter, despite much effort, but we did finally pick up Grey Wagtail and Goldcrest. Whilst looking for the wagtail, we had our second flat tyre — fortunately Russ had a spare tube and quickly helped fix John's rear wheel (thanks Russ!).

We finally headed back into Maldon, with nothing new, and through the Prom Park, dodging the crowds. Emma Neave-Webb then joined us and, fuelled by more tea, our last few hours were spent along Southey Creek. Although our hit rate was now averaging only one or two new birds an hour, persistence brought us further additions, such as a late Common Gull and a couple of Wigeon. At last, after getting on for 16 hours in the field, and with a large amount of wet weather heading towards us, it was time to call it a day. Fortunately our earlier success with owls meant there was no need to chase them up after dark.

The final team total of 105 was at the time our record Maldon day list total and all achieved by pedal power alone. Just a pity the sea wall footpaths aren't that bit easier on the saddle! We have beaten it only once since, on 7th May the following year with a score of 108, though that was with the help of a car.

Chelmer and Blackwater Navigation

Recommended Local Wildlife Walks

With the sea walls and a diverse network of public footpaths there are many ways to explore the countryside around Maldon, Heybridge and surrounding parishes. The following suggested routes are selected to showcase some of the best locations for wildlife.

Some of the paths can be muddy at times, particularly in the winter, when walking boots or wellies would be recommended!

Location of local wildlife walks around Maldon and Heybridge. The red circles mark the starting/finishing points

Walk 1 • Heybridge circuit from Daisy Lane Car Park (distance c4 km)

This walk starts at Heybridge Locks and provides great views across the head of the estuary, while also giving you a chance to enjoy the wildlife of the pits themselves. Birds can include Cuckoo, Common Tern and the Black-headed Gull colony in the summer and wintering ducks and Bearded Tit in the winter.

- Park in Daisy Lane Car Park TL870069
- Turn left on to the path and walk south-east along the canal
- Cross the canal at the lock gates and walk up to the sea wall
- Head right along the seawall footpath as it leads clockwise around the Gravel Pits
- You can walk for a short while and turn back or else carry on all the way to the end of the pits and then walk through the housing estate and then over the foot bridge to walk back along the canal
- By Heybridge Lock there are two pubs and a tea room for refreshments

Walk 2 • Sea wall walk to Mundon Sluice (distance c5 km)

Good all year round but especially in the winter when the Brent Geese, the wintering ducks and waders and the relative solitude can combine to create a truly wild experience.

- Park in the Promenade Park TL863065
- Follow the coastal path south-east past the sailing club and onto the sea wall by the recycling centre. If the tide is coming in there may be close views of waders on the mud — Black-tailed Godwit, Redshank, Dunlin — and the wintering flock of Golden Plover is often roosting on the dredgings. In recent years, good views of Avocet have been possible
- Carry on along the sea wall and stop to scan the Dump Pool on your right, where there are likely to be Common Teal and often a Little Egret and, if water levels are low, a chance of Green Sandpiper and other waders
- Following the sea wall, you reach two kissing gates, as the path crosses the track down to the Northey Island causeway
- Keep on the sea wall and after a couple of fields you will reach Limbourne Creek on your right. Brent Geese could be in any of the fields or, depending on the tides, out on Southey Creek, the channel between you and the island. In spring and autumn look out for Wheatear here
- Keep on going and you will reach the sluice. From here there is a good view across Southey Creek and further downstream across the Blackwater, with Osea Island in the background
- This is the best place for seeing Pintail alongside the other wildfowl: Common Teal, Wigeon and Common Shelduck and a possibility of grebes and even a distant diver, if it's high tide
- To return, simply retrace your steps but keep a watchful eye out for raptors. In winter there could be a Short-eared Owl. At any time of year, there is a reasonable

chance of seeing a Marsh Harrier or Peregrine and, if you are there towards dusk, the possibility of a Barn Owl hunting along the borrow dykes

- Refreshments available at cafés in the park or at the pubs on the Hythe

Walk 3 • Canal-side walk at Beeleigh

A scenic walk that gives opportunities to see riverside birds and, in summer, an impressive variety of dragon and damselflies.

Walking route:

- Walk out from Maldon along the north side of river taking the sea wall path that runs beside the Tesco supermarket car park TL849075 (in summer, warblers in the reedbed; in winter, Common Teal and possible waders on the river)
- Continue along edge of Maldon Golf Course (possible thrushes, Jay)
- Cross onto path to go over main weir
- From main weir, watch the Mute Swan and, depending on tide, water level and season, look out for Grey Wagtail, Common Teal, Little Egret and possible Common Sandpiper
- Follow path and take track to left to Beeleigh footbridge (Reed and Cetti's Warbler likely, Kingfisher possible)

Then either:

- Continue through kissing gate past Beeleigh Mill along Abbey Turning
- Turn left at wide track, pass Beeleigh Abbey and follow footpaths back to Maldon

Or:

- Head back to towpath, turn left and, crossing lock, head up and down canal as time allows (lots of dragon and damselflies in summer)
- As you head along canal look out for Kestrel, Common Buzzard and, in spring, listen out for warblers and possibility of Turtle Dove and Nightingale
- Walk back to Maldon along canal towpath and cross footbridge just before Tesco car park to return to Maldon (more chance of dragon and damselflies)

Driving route:

- Drive out of Maldon on the Langford Road (B1019) and take the Maldon Golf Course entrance road on the left just before the Museum of Power
- Follow entrance road to parking area just before bridge TL840084. Note the land is private and free parking in recent years has been made available only due to

generosity of the landowner. (In winter there have often been flocks of Siskin in the Alder either side of the entrance road)

- Walk over the bridge and explore the weir and canal as per above walking route

Walk 4 • Chigborough Lakes Essex Wildlife Trust Reserve

- The main car park is on Chigborough Road about $^3/_4$ mile north from the junction with Goldhanger Road (Grid Reference TL 878087)

- There is a map on a board in the car park to assist in your orientation. The main lakes are in two groups — to see all of them entails a figure of eight shaped route

- Throughout the reserve there are occasional spots where you can stop and look across the different areas of water. In summer there are both Great Crested and Little Grebe besides the regular Mute Swan, Mallard, Tufted Duck, Coot, Moorhen and Cormorant. In winter there are additional ducks to be seen: Gadwall, Shoveler, Common Teal and Common Pochard, plus chances of others such as Goldeneye and Wigeon

- Throughout the reserve there are various woodland birds to be seen: Great, Blue, and Long-tailed Tit, Great Spotted and Green Woodpecker, Jay, Treecreeper, Wren. Bullfinch is regular. In summer, various warblers can be heard and seen. Cetti's Warbler and Chiffchaff can be encountered all year round. In winter, Goldcrest and Woodcock occur; Firecrest is possible. Birds of prey include Tawny Owl, Sparrowhawk and Common Buzzard, with Hobby often seen in summer

- The heronry is at the extreme distance from the Chigborough Road car park — if time is tight you might prefer to park in the layby on Scraley Road and head to the gate just inside the reserve at TL 870089 to view. This is also the best place from which to view the Jackdaw roost

- The entrance to the footpath that runs past the pits at Lofts Farm is on Scraley Road, just north of the gate, on the other side of the road

Causeway to Osea Island at high tide (Carla Davis)

A Manifesto for Maldon's Wildlife

Throughout the preceding chapters, mention has been made of opportunities to help ensure the survival of our wildlife into the future. Here, to end the book, they are consolidated into a set of twelve recommendations for those who want to help:

- Make your views known to local councillors (and Minister of Parliament for bigger issues)

- Push for new building developments to include provisions to preserve habitat features, landscape sympathetically with native plant species and provide extra green spaces and other mitigations to compensate for lost habitat

- Press the council to ensure developers fully deliver on all required actions and on any additional agreements

- Require new builds to incorporate sustainability features such as solar panels and turbines as well as swift and bat boxes

- Press the council to establish Local Nature Reserves to protect key locations

- Differentiate between public spaces for dog walking, football, picnics and drones, and places where wildlife can be allowed some peace

- Avoid disturbance of waders and wildfowl on the saltmarsh

- Support farmers who use wildlife friendly methods

- Encourage wildflower verges and wildlife friendly mowing and hedge-trimming regimes

- Create wildlife-friendly gardens, avoid use of chemical insecticides and herbicides

- Join conservation groups such as the Essex Wildlife Trust to help support their land aquisition and management activities and their work with local autorities to protect key habitats

- Celebrate our wildlife and spread the word!

Whether young or old, all needs looking after...

One of the oldest inhabitants of Maldon, this majestic Sessile Oak, with a girth of around seven metres, has stood by the entrance drive to Great Beeleigh Farm for hundreds of years.

A surprise find as this book was being finished was a group of Lizard Orchid along the sea wall at Heybridge Pits. June 2021 (JB)

Only the second record ever in Essex of this rare plant, it is protected by Schedule 8 of the Wildlife & Countryside Bill. Nevertheless care needs to be taken to ensure it is not damaged by the annual mowing regime of the sea wall by the Environment Agency before it has finished flowering.

REFERENCES

Essex Natural Histories

Miller Christy, "*The Birds of Essex, A Contribution to the Natural History of the County*", 1890, Essex Field Club

Henry Laver, "*The Mammals, Reptiles and Fishes of Essex*", 1898, Essex Field Club

William Glegg, "*A History of the Birds of Essex*", 1929, H.F & G Witherby

Robert Hudson & Geoffrey A Pyman, "*A Guide to the Birds of Essex*", 1968, Essex Birdwatching & Preservation Society

Dr Simon Cox, "*A New Guide to the Birds of Essex*", 1984, Essex Birdwatching & Preservation Society

Simon Wood, "*The Birds of Essex*", 2007, Helm

The Essex Bird Reports — the annual report of accepted bird records for the county published by the Essex Birdwatching Society

John Dobson & Darren Tansley, "*Mammals of Essex*", updated edition, 2014, Essex Field Club

David Corke, "*The Butterflies of Essex*", 1997, Lopinga Books

Ted Benton & John Dobson, "*The Dragonflies of Essex*", 2007, The Essex Field Club & Lopinga Books

Ted Benton, "*The Bumblebees of Essex*", 2000, Lopinga Books

Books on Maldon

E. A. Fitch, "*Maldon and the River Blackwater*", 1894, Gowers

Ian Linton, "*The Book of Maldon*", 1984, Barracuda Books

Stephen P. Nunn, "*Maldon & Heybridge Through Time*", 2012, Ambersley Publishing

Specific references

Chapter 1 — Setting the Scene

The Domesday Book, 1086, accessed from http://opendomesday.org/

Maldon Archaeological Group, "*Maeldune, Light on Maldon's Distant Past*", 1992, available online

Chapter 2 — Geology and Early Natural History

Dr Francis Pryor, *"The Making of the British Landscape: How We Have Transformed the Land, from Prehistory to Today"*, 2010, Allen Lane

Lofts Farm Gravel Pit, Geology Site Account, Essex Field Club (accessed from Essex Field Club website)

Johnstone, C. and Albarella, U., *"The Late Iron Age and Romano-British mammal and bird bone assemblage from Elms Farm, Heybridge, Essex*, in M. Atkinson and S.J. Preston *Heybridge: A Late Iron Age and Roman Settlement, Excavations at Elms Farm 1993–5"*, 2015, Internet Archaeology 40

Chapter 3 — Maldon Now

Daniel Defoe, "*Tour Through the Eastern Counties of England*", 1722

Blackwater Estuary Ramsar Statement, Version 3.0, JNCC, 13/06/2008

Simon Wood, *"The Wildlife of Heybridge Gravel Pit"*, (work in prep.)

David N. Williams, "*The Water Supply to Essex and Beyond*", a web resource located at essexwatersupply.com

Chigborough Lakes Visitor Guide, Essex Wildlife Trust

"RSPB Big Garden Birdwatch Results 2015", March 2016, Royal Society for the Protection of Birds

Chapter 4 — The Main Players

Wernham, C.V., Toms, M.P., Clark, J.A., Siriwardena, G.M. & Baillie, S.R. (eds), *"The Migration Atlas: Movements of the birds of Britain and Ireland"*, 2002, T. & A.D. Poyser

Jim Flegg, *"Time to Fly — Exploring Bird Migration"*, 2004, British Trust for Ornithology

Chapter 5 — Wildlife Through the Year

Dawn Balmer, Simon Gillings, Brian Caffrey, Bob Swann, Iain Downie; Rob Fuller, *"Bird Atlas 2007–11: The Breeding and Wintering Birds of Britain and Ireland"*, 2013, British Trust for Ornithology

J. A. Baker, *"The Peregrine"*, 1967, HarperCollins

Dr Moss Taylor, *"The Polish Swan in Britain and Ireland",* British Birds Vol 111, Jan 2018

Chapter 7 — Mammals

Barker, J., Seymour, A., Mowat, S., Debney, A., *"Thames Harbour Seal Conservation Project"*, 2014, UK & Europe Conservation Programme Report, Zoological Society of London

Record of Northern Bottlenose Whale included in Thomas Pennant, *"British Zoology"*, 1769, London (Under Class IV: Fish)

Chapter 9 — Invertebrates

"The State of the UK's Butterflies 2015", 2015, Butterfly Conservation and the Centre for Ecology & Hydrology, Wareham, Dorset

Chapter 10 — Plants

"Climate change: The UK's wild Flowers are on the move", on-line article on Plantlife website accessed Oct 2020

Joanna Bromley, Ben McCarthy, Catharine Shellswell, *"Managing Grassland Road Verges"*, 2019, Plantlife

"Tree Trail, Promenade Park", booklet published by Maldon District Council

Chapter 11 — Introductions and Escapees

"*National Gamebird Census*", Gamebird & Wildlife Conservation Trust

"Key tree pests and diseases" & linked pages, on Woodland Trust website accessed Oct 2020

Chapter 12— Changing Populations

"The State of the UK's Birds 2020", 2020, RSPB et al.

UK Population data – Office of National Statistics

"The Breeding Bird Survey 2018", BTO Research Report 717, 2019, British Trust for Ornithology

Mark Eaton, Mark Holling and the Rare Breeding Birds Panel, *"Rare breeding birds in the UK in 2018"*, published in British Birds Vol 113, Dec 2020

"PDSA Animal Wellbeing Report 2020", 2020, People's Dispensary for Sick Animals

"The State of Britain's Larger Moths 2021", 2021, Butterfly Conservation

"A review of the status of Microlepidoptera in Britain", 2012, Butterfly Conservation

"Waterbirds in the UK 2018/19, the Annual Report of the Wetland Bird Survey", 2020, British Trust for Ornithology

"*Conservation Status Review 7: Report on the conservation status of migratory waterbirds in the agreement area*", May 2018, published by the secretariat of the Agreement on the Conservation of African-Eurasian Migratory Waterbirds

Chapter 13 — The Future

Derek Winstanley, Robert Spencer and Kenneth Williamson, "*Where Have All the Whitethroats Gone?*", 1974, Bird Study 21:1

"*2019 State of Nature Report*", 2019, The State of Nature Partnership

Intergovernmental Panel on Climate Change, "*Summary for Policymakers of IPCC Special Report on Global Warming of 1.5°C approved by governments*", 2018, accessed from IPCC website

Long term flood risk taken from UK Government Flood Warning Information Service, *https://flood-warning-information.service.gov.uk*

Dave Slater, "*Update on licences for control of lesser black-backed gulls and herring gulls and of birds on or close to protected sites*", Natural England, Apr 2020

Chapter 15 — A Miscellany

Ken Stubbings, "*Here's Good Luck to the Pint Pot — a brief history of Maldon's Inns, Alehouses and Breweries*", 1988, Kelvin Brown Publications

Common Poppy in a wheat field near Beeleigh Abbey

CREDITS AND ACKNOWLEDGEMENTS

Acknowledgements

This book has only been possible to be as comprehensive as it is through the support provided by a great many wildlife enthusiasts, from Essex and beyond, who have readily contributed records, knowledge and anecdotes to this venture. Particular thanks are due to: Dave Appleton, Mike Bailey, Sarah Binnie (Essex Wildlife Trust Biological Records Centre), Maureen Bissell, Laura Cheskin (Maldon Wildlife Rescue), Dr Simon Cox, Mark Curteis (Chelmsford Museum), Adrian Dally, Carla Davis, John Dobson, Bart Ebbinge, Neil Frost (Chelmer Canal Trust), Tim Gardiner, Richard Gilbert & David Mason (National Trust), Steve Grimwade, Anthony Harbott, Tony Kennelly, Nic Lindsell, David Low, Phil Luke, Peter Potts, Roy Read, Daryl Rhymes, Tim Sapsford (Essex Bat Group), Dr Moss Taylor and Chris Tyas.

Any errors are down to the lead author, who also apologises if any of the grammar and style have jarred. After 35 years of working in a corporate environment, where accuracy and succinctness took priority over literary merit, I have had to re-learn how to write prose and punctuate!

Thanks too to Mike Dawson, Kaarin Wall and Andy Stoddart, for patiently helping me scale the initial rungs of the book publication learning ladder.

And of course many thanks to the rest of the patch team: Simon, Russell, Emma and Simon. The more you look at nature, the more questions arise, and it is wonderful to have people around who can help answer them for you and support you on your journey to enlightenment.

Finally, on a personal note, I am forever grateful for the support and company of my wonderful wife, Jan, and to my children, Iain and Rebecca, who are a constant inspiration and reminder that we need to look after our wildlife so it will be there for future generations to appreciate and benefit from. Thank you Iain, for the music and for keeping me on my toes, and to Becca for filling our house with art!

John Buchanan
Maldon, May 2021

Black-tailed Godwit, Heybridge Pits, Apr 2016 (SW)

Photographic credits

Huge thanks are given to all who have generously contributed the photographs that have so enriched this book. All have been taken within our Maldon patch. Unfortunately, for some, the wildlife subjects were not willing to stay still and pose at close range for their moment of fame but these photos have been included nonetheless as a record of what can be seen here. The photographs are generally credited to the photographers within the captions. Any not credited in this way are attributable to John Buchanan. Note all copyrights are retained by the original photographers.

The full list of photographers is: Maureen Bissell, John Buchanan (JB), Paul Chamberlain, Chelmer Canal Trust, Andy Cook, Carla Davis, Barwoilt Ebbinge Research Team, Graham Ekins, Tom Harris, Adrian Kettle, Cindy Lawes, Russell Neave (RN), Peter Potts, Sarah Sapsford, Simon Patient (SP), South Woodham Coastguard Rescue Team, Simon Wood (SW) & Stephen Shelley.

The maps used on pages 7, 13 & 201 are based on maps available under the Open Data License © OpenStreetMap contributors.

APPENDICES

APPENDIX I

Overview of Birds Recorded within the Maldon Study Area
(including selected past records)

Overall list

During the period 2000–2020, **238** different species of bird were reliably recorded within the Maldon patch.

Following a thorough review of historic records we have established an all-time list of species found and reliably identified in the area totalling **265**.

Seasonal statuses (2000–2020)

(If status changed during the period, the status noted is the status in 2020)

Regular species (expected to occur every year):

Seen all year round:	79
Seen mainly in summer:	15
Seen mainly in winter:	40
Seen mainly on passage (on migration):	22
Total regular species:	**156**

Species that are <u>not</u> expected to be seen annually: (of which 36 were recorded only once)	82
Total species recorded during period:	**238**

Breeding statuses (2000–2020)

Breeding regularly at end of study period:	86
Have bred during period but not regularly:	15
Total species bred during period:	**101**
Possible breeding but not confirmed:	4

A full list of species recorded is included in Appendix IV

Past records

Interesting records of rare/ scarce birds prior to our study period include:

Purple Heron — first Essex record: one shot, "in a wood near Maldon", 2nd week Apr 1839

Rose-coloured Starling — one shot, Maldon/ Heybridge, c1870 (now in Chelmsford Museum) and another, Heybridge, 29th–30th Dec 1889

Hoopoe — one shot, on border between Woodham Mortimer & Danbury, 20th Sept 1880 and then one in modern times at Chigborough Lakes, 29th Mar 1997

Stone Curlew — four, Heybridge, 11th Dec 1890

Corncrake — flock seen and three were shot, Northey Island, 20–25th Sept 1897

Manx Shearwater — one between Mill Beach & Goldhanger, 14th Sept 1953

White-rumped Sandpiper — one, Heybridge Pits, 31st Aug 1972

Kentish Plover — one, Heybridge Pits, 19th Oct 1969 and another 27th July 1974

Pectoral Sandpiper — one, Heybridge Pits, 27st Aug–20th Sept 1973 and another 31st Aug–8th Sept 1981

Ring-necked Duck — male, Heybridge Pits, 27th Apr–5th May 1979

Wilson's Phalarope — one, Chigborough Lakes, 6–10th Sept 1980

Night Heron — adult, Northey Island, 25th Oct 1980

Caspian Tern — one, Heybridge Pits, 20th–22nd June 1981

Dark-breasted Barn Owl — one, Northey Island, 18th Jan 1982

Leach's Petrel — one, Heybridge Pits, 6th Nov 1983 (in fog)

Ortolan Bunting — one, Heybridge Pits, 3rd May 1984

Long-billed Dowitcher — one, Heybridge Pits, 29th Sept–6th Oct 1985

Red-backed Shrike — male, Heybridge Pits, 8th July 1987 (only record since breeding ceased)

Richard's Pipit — one, South House Farm, 21st–28th Oct 1988

Willow Tit — two, Chigborough Lakes, 24th Mar & 1st Apr 1991 (last known records)

Yellow Wagtail — male with features of Black-headed race (though potentially an intergrade), near Brick House Farm, 24th May–24th June 1999

Montagu's Harrier — one, Brick House Farm, 25th May 1999

White-winged Black Tern— one, Heybridge Pits, 30th Aug– 3rd Sept 1999

APPENDIX II

Breeding Bird Species Lost and Gained within the Study Period (with particular reference to those of UK conservation importance)

The UK Red Lists identify those species of wildlife concern from a national perspective. They are coordinated by the Joint Nature Conservation Committee (JNCC), the body established by the UK Government to advise on UK-wide and international nature conservation. In the case of birds the list is maintained by the British Trust for Ornithology. The latest edition, 'Birds of Conservation Concern 4', was published in December 2015.

The charts on the following pages identify the sixteen Red-listed species from this list that were still regularly breeding around Maldon in 2020 as well as identifying those species recently lost as breeders, those at most risk and then the breeding species we have gained.

Of the species lost, the Red-listed Spotted Flycatcher and the Meadow Pipit were both an integral part of our avifauna so their disappearance is a big loss. Ringed Plover and Stonechat could perhaps be best thought of as having been just occasional breeders, nesting only at Heybridge Pits. Nevertheless their loss is still to be regretted and no doubt due to the various housing developments and increased footfall that the area has suffered. Ringed Plover was still breeding just outside the patch in 2020, at Mundon Stone Point.

The chart identifies a worrying twelve species that the team feel are of risk of being lost in the next few years if there is no change in their fortunes. These include nine Red-listed species. Indeed, further surveying in 2021 suggests that Willow Warbler and Lapwing have already ceased to breed in the patch. A further development noted in 2021 appears to be a collapse in House Martin numbers, perhaps due to bad weather stalling their migration north in the spring.

Of the birds that bred for the first time during 2000–2020, two are on the UK Red List — Herring Gull and Black Redstart. It looks as though Herring Gull is now well established, with a vibrant colony in the industrial area, assuming no attempt is made by the landowners to move them on. However the Black Redstart breeding record in 2020 may end up as an isolated event as Maldon is so distant from the species' stronghold in East London or any of the pairs on the coast.

Breeding bird species recently lost from the Maldon Study Area and the status of those at risk

Species lost as breeding species during study period 2000-2020

Stonechat		Bred Heybridge Pits in 2003, 2004 and possibly 2005 but not since
Ruddy Duck		Not native to UK — population culled due to perceived impacts on other species Used to breed regularly; last local sighting at Heybridge Pits, 2008
Ringed Plover		Bred regularly at Heybridge Pits in 1960s & 70s but only sporadically thereafter. Last bred there 2009 Still a pair just outside study area at Mundon Stone Point, 2020
Spotted Flycatcher	R	Last known breeding pair at Beeleigh Abbey in 2016
Meadow Pipit		Following decline, no singing birds found in 2020

Species with a significant risk of being lost in the near future

Lesser Spotted Woodpecker	R	Only recent breeding season records have been single birds at Hazeleigh Wood
Willow Warbler		Majority of singing birds in spring now are just passing through (None recorded breeding in 2021)
Lapwing	R	In 2020 just two pairs breeding Lawling Creek, a decline from previous years (None recorded breeding in 2021)
Grey Partridge	R	Any remaining pairs are thought to be a result of game releases
Redshank		In 2020 four pairs recorded breeding Lawling Creek but gone from sites where bred previously
Turtle Dove	R	UK population collapsing due to multiple factors Less than a handful of isolated pairs left in study area
Yellow Wagtail	R	In steady decline as a local breeding species
Grey Wagtail	R	Only one breeding pair (at Beeleigh)
Garden Warbler		Numbers erratic, gone from some regular sites in recent years
Nightingale	R	UK population declining generally. Additional risk to local population due to majority being concentrated in just one site
Yellowhammer	R	In steady decline as breeding species and reducing numbers in winter
Corn Bunting	R	In steady decline as breeding species though considerable number still winter
Swift		Significant national decline reflected in fewer birds being seen around the town
House Martin		Significant national decline. Numbers appeared to have collapsed locally in 2021, with many regular breeding sites not being used

Red-listed species still with a significant breeding presence

Cuckoo	R	Still regular at a number of traditional locations, both wetland and farmland
Skylark	R	Still regular but declining in the face of monoculture fields and lack of undisturbed nesting sites
Linnet	R	Still regular as a breeding species in suitable habitat
Mistle Thrush	R	Still regular at a number of traditional locations
Song Thrush	R	Currently regular and widespread, having recovered somewhat from previous decline
House Sparrow	R	Still fairly common and widespread
Starling	R	Still regular and widespread as a breeding species

Bird species that have recently colonised/ re-colonised the Maldon Study Area

	Status in UK/ Essex	Occurrence in Maldon Study Area
Species breeding for the first time during late 20th Century		
Greylag Goose		Gradually spreading — by the 1980s they were already breeding on gravel pits in the area around Maldon
Canada Goose		Gradually spreading — by the 1980s they were already breeding on gravel pits in the area around Maldon
Egyptian Goose	First bred in Essex in 1979 (Fishers Green & Holyfield Marsh)	First bred at Chigborough in 1998 Steady increase in numbers — started breeding Lofts Farm 2011 and Heybridge 2016
Collared Dove	First arrived in UK in the 1950s, with the first Essex record at Tollesbury in 1957 Has since spread prolifically throughout the county and nationwide	Now fully established throughout the district and one of the commonest and familiar garden birds
Species breeding for the first time 2000-2020 that are now fully established		
Little Egret	First bred in UK in 1996 (Dorset) First bred in Essex in 2000 with seven pairs in south of county	First bred at Chigborough Lakes EWT Reserve in 2003 and has bred there continuously since
Cormorant	First contemporary inland breeding in UK was at Abberton Reservoir, Essex in 1981	After roosting in the area from the 1990s, first bred at Lofts Farm in 2010 and has bred either there or Chigborough Lakes continuously since
Herring Gull **R**	First bred in Essex in 1992 (Foulness)	Year of first local breeding not recorded but nesting on industrial buildings in Heybridge by 2013 at least and each year subsequently
Lesser Black-backed Gull	First bred in Essex in 1991 (Hanningfield)	Year of first local breeding not recorded but nesting on industrial buildings in Heybridge by 2013 at least and each year subsequently
Cetti's Warbler	First bred in UK in 1972 (Kent) First Essex records in 1976 (Berwick Ponds)	First local breeding season presence at Heybridge Pits in 2000 and spread widely in the area since. Exact date of first breeding not known
Birds that bred for the first time 2000-2020 but are not fully established		
Cattle Egret	First bred in UK in 2008 (Somerset)	First bred Chigborough Lakes EWT Reserve in 2019 (first Essex record) Adults & juvenile also recorded in 2020
Gadwall	First bred in Essex in 1921 (along the Crouch) but colonisation of Essex slow, with Hanningfield & Abberton holding core of population till 1990s	Adults with young seen Chigborough Lakes EWT 2017 & 2019 in (Pairs had summered previously at Heybridge and Lofts Farm)
Little Ringed Plover	First bred in UK in 1938 (Tring, Herts) First bred in Essex in 1947 (Girling) and has bred in Essex continually since 1954	Three pairs at Heybridge Pits in 2007 is the only confirmed breeding record though summered in previous years
Ring-necked Parakeet	Given large populations in London/ Kent, spread into Essex has been slow Double figure flocks were seen in Metropolitan Essex from 1971	Pair bred in 2012 in a tree at Fitch's Crescent — isolated record but likely future colonist as preferred garden/ parkland habitat seems available
Bearded Tit	First confirmed contemporary breeding in Essex at Old Hall (1962)	Two pairs bred east of Osea Causeway in 2018; probably bred Heybridge Pits in 2006, 2019 & 2020
Black Redstart **R**	UK population in general has shown signs of gradual increase in recent years	Pair bred by Chandlers Quay in 2020. At least one chick fledged. May also have bred in 2019.
Previously lost species returning to breed 2000-2020		
Avocet	Ceased breeding in UK by mid 1840s First contemporary breeding in Essex in 1944 (Langenhoe)	First local breeding in 2006 in Heybridge Pits and has bred there subsequently (May have bred previously in 18th century)
Common Buzzard	Ten breeding pairs in Essex in 2002. Rapid expansion — by 2013 was the most widespread bird of prey in Essex	First local breeding in 2014 in Hazeleigh Wood Multiple pairs now breeding around the study area
Common Pochard	From a long term low level, Essex breeding population began steadily expanding in 1960s	Pair bred in 2014 at Heybridge Pits and have bred there since as well as at Chigborough Lakes EWT and Flight Pond by Mundon Sluice (Breeding recorded at Northey Island in 1887)
Teal	Has bred in Essex long term but in very low numbers.	One pair bred in 2005 at Heybridge Pits — isolated record (Bred on Northey Island in 19th century)
Nuthatch	Presumed to have bred in area historically	Seen in Hazeleigh area in 2015 and in subsequent years, including sighting of juvenile Recorded breeding in Kent Wood in 2020

R = UK Red-listed due to severe long-term national breeding population and/ or range decline

Bird species with potential to colonise but not yet proven to breed

	Status in UK/ Essex	Occurrence in Maldon Study Area
Other previously lost breeding species with potential to return in near future		
Red Kite	First contemporary breeding in Essex in 2016 as part of expansion throughout the UK following successful re-introduction schemes	First contemporary local sighting in 2002 Increasing numbers now seen in study area each year and in all seasons — expected soon to start breeding in local woods
Raven	First contemporary Essex breeding in 2016 as part of natural population/ range expansion; multiple Essex nesting sites in 2020	First contemporary local sighting in 2019 Increased sightings/ breeding in neighborouring districts suggest that Maldon Study Area could be colonised soon
Birds showing signs of breeding for the first time 2000-2020 but no actual breeding took place/ proven		
Black-necked Grebe	First successfully bred in Essex in 2001	1–2 birds have stayed for extended periods at Lofts Farm, where habitat looks ideal, however breeding did not take place (site prone to disturbance from fishing activities)
Wigeon	First bred in Essex in 1929 but only erratically since	Pair summered at Lofts Farm in 2001 and at Lawling Creek in 2005
Shoveler	Has bred in Essex long term in small numbers	Pair summered at Lofts Farm in 2001
Marsh Harrier	May have bred historically First contemporary Essex breeding in 1992 (Foulness); now breeding at mutiple Essex sites	Pairs seen displaying in summer
Mediterranean Gull	First pure breeding in Essex in 1990 (in prior years it was suspected there had been hybrid pairings between Mediterranean and Black-headed Gull)	One, or occasionally two, pairs have summered in Maldon since 2012, often joining Black-headed Gulls at colony in Heybridge Pits but so far have not actually bred
Firecrest	First confirmed breeding in Essex in 1980 (Harlow Woods)	Increasing sightings, including singing males in spring

↑ Black-necked Grebe, Lofts Farm, Mar 2010 (SP)

A potential colonist of the gravel pits.

→ Male Marsh Harrier, nr Osea Road, Apr 2018 (SW)

Could breed in reed beds if not too much disturbance.

APPENDIX III

Changes to Status of Wintering Wildfowl and Wader Populations on the Blackwater Estuary

As explained in the main text, the estuary at Maldon has a vital role as a passage and wintering site for migrant wildfowl and wader species.

Monthly counts of different sections are carried out for the British Trust for Ornithology's Wetland Bird Survey (WeBS). However due to the frequent movements of birds up and down the estuary, to understand overall population fluctuations it is easiest to consider the Blackwater Estuary numbers as a whole. (This approach also aligns to the fact that from a conservation perspective, all the international and national designations for the Blackwater Estuary consider it as a single entity.)

The chart below looks at total numbers and recent changes for the 20 most numerous wildfowl and wader species that currently winter on the Blackwater.

	1 Blackwater Current 5yr Mean	2 Blackwater 10 yr change %	3 UK 10 yr change %	4 International Latest overall assessment
Species/ Form				
Dunlin	16,653	44%	0%	Stable
Knot	15,062	230%	-10%	Stable
Golden Plover	9,186	-1%	-31%	Stable
Brent Goose (Dark-bellied)	8,935	26%	5%	Stable
Lapwing	6,878	-15%	-20%	Decreasing
Wigeon	5,285	-18%	-3%	Decreasing
Teal	4,614	198%	14%	Increasing
Grey Plover	3,797	-2%	-20%	Decreasing
Shelduck	3,187	64%	-13%	Stable
Redshank	3,099	1%	-9%	Decreasing
Black-tailed Godwit (Icelandic)	3,019	55%	31%	Increasing
Curlew	1,544	-1%	-21%	Decreasing
Oystercatcher	1,193	4%	-12%	Stable
Turnstone	716	12%	-25%	Increasing
Pintail	699	91%	-29%	Stable
Avocet	683	71%	24%	Increasing
Mallard	479	-17%	-12%	Stable
Ringed Plover	434	-9%	-23%	Decreasing
Bar-tailed Godwit	415	253%	8%	Increasing
Goldeneye	134	26%	-31%	Stable

Sources of data:

1: Mean of peak WeBS counts for whole Blackwater Estuary over last 5 winters 2014/15–2018/19

2: % change vs same data from 10 years previously, ie over period 1994/5–2018/19

3: As 1 & 2 but considering % change for total UK counts over same period

1, 2 & 3 all retrieved from the WeBS report: Waterbirds in the UK 2018/19

4: Latest international population trends taken from the 2018 7th edition of the Conservation Status Report of the Agreement on the Conservation of African-Eurasian Migratory Waterbirds

The numbers on the chart highlighted in red signify population decreases. There are many factors playing into the counts, so the numbers should not be taken as precise — the data is shown just to give an indication of how much change is taking place. (More details of the factors involved, including changes in year to year coverage, are included in the annual Waterbirds in the UK WeBS reports.)

It is clear that across the UK, numbers of a large number of species have been dropping. It is possible that for some, there are drops due to changes in wintering location, with climate changes meaning that more birds winter on the continent, remaining closer to their breeding areas as there is less need to move to avoid severe weather. However the data on global changes in the right hand column shows that most of these species are subject to global declines.

Many of these species are truly international, with different populations using different flyways to winter in different regions for the world. For both the Godwits listed, although the local forms may be doing comparatively well, their populations in other parts of the world are suffering. While Icelandic Black-tailed Godwit are currently increasing, the main European population is on the decline. For Bar-tailed Godwit, the population most in trouble is the one that migrates along the East Asian-Australasian Flyway due to loss of habitat at critical stopover sites in the Yellow Sea.

Populations of Curlew and Lapwing are also of international concern, with both sadly declining in the UK and locally as well.

There is more discussion of this data in Chapter 12 of the main text but the key conclusion is very apparent — in a time of generally reducing populations, the relative importance of the Blackwater Estuary within a UK context is increasing.

Note: Wetland Bird Survey (WeBS) data included here is from *"Waterbirds in the UK 2018/19"* © copyright and database right 2020. WeBS is a partnership jointly funded by the BTO, RSPB and JNCC, in association with WWT, with fieldwork conducted by volunteers.

APPENDIX IV

Full list of Bird Species Recorded within the Maldon Study Area

A list of all the species considered to have been reliably recorded in a wild state within our patch — the Maldon Study Area — along with their occurrence pattern and breeding status during the 2000–2020 study period:

Definitions of occurrence	Definitions of breeding status
For species seen 2000–2020:	**For species breeding 2000–2020:**
All= seen all months	**Regular**= breeding regularly at end of study period
S= seen during Summer months	**Irregular**= bred irregularly during period
W= seen during Winter months	**Possible**= possibly bred during period, not confirmed
P= seen on Passage (spring/ autumn)	**For species believed only to have bred historically:**
(Upper case= main season of occurence)	**Historic**= only recorded breeding prior to 2000
Rare= not expected to occur annually	**?Historic**= breeding assumed but not proven
Once= recorded only once during study period	
For species only recorded historically:	
Historic= only recorded prior to 2000	

SPECIES RECORDED (distinctive subspecies in italics)	Occurrence	Breeding Status	SPECIES RECORDED (distinctive subspecies in italics)	Occurrence	Breeding Status
Dark-bellied Brent Goose *(bernicla)*	W, p		Grey Partridge	All	Regular
Pale-bellied Brent Goose (hrota)	Rare		Quail	Rare	Possible
Black Brant (nigricans)	Rare		(Common) Pheasant	All	Regular
Red-breasted Goose	Historic		Nightjar	Once	
Canada Goose	All	Regular	Alpine Swift	Once	
Barnacle Goose	Rare		(Common) Swift	S	Regular
Greylag Goose	All	Regular	Cuckoo	S	Regular
Pink-footed Goose	Rare		Rock Dove (Feral Pigeon)	All	Regular
Tundra Bean Goose	Rare		Stock Dove	All	Regular
(Russian) White-fronted Goose *(albifrons)*	Rare		Woodpigeon	All	Regular
Mute Swan	All	Regular	Turtle Dove	S	Regular
Bewick's Swan	Rare		Collared Dove	All	Regular
Whooper Swan	Rare		Water Rail	W, s	Regular
Egyptian Goose	All	Regular	Corncrake	Historic	
(Common) Shelduck	All	Regular	Spotted Crake	Once	
Mandarin Duck	Rare		Moorhen	All	Regular
Baikal Teal	Once		Coot	All	Regular
Garganey	P		(Common) Crane	Rare	
Shoveler	W		Little Grebe	All	Regular
Gadwall	W, s	Irregular	Red-necked Grebe	Rare	
(Eurasian) Wigeon	W		Great Crested Grebe	All	Regular
Mallard	All	Regular	Slavonian Grebe	W	
Pintail	W		Black-necked Grebe	Rare	Possible
(Common) Teal	W	Irregular	Stone-curlew	Historic	
Green-Winged Teal	Once		Oystercatcher	All	Regular
Red-crested Pochard	Rare		Black-Winged Stilt	Once	
(Common) Pochard	W, s	Regular	Avocet	W, s	Irregular
Ferruginous Duck	Once		Lapwing	W	Irregular
Ring-necked Duck	Once		Golden Plover	W	
Tufted Duck	All	Regular	American Golden Plover	Once	
Scaup	W		Grey Plover	W, p	
Eider	Rare		Ringed Plover	W, p	Irregular
Velvet Scoter	Rare		Little Ringed Plover	P	Irregular
Common Scoter	W		Kentish Plover	Historic	
Long-tailed Duck	Rare		Whimbrel	P	
Goldeneye	W		Curlew	W	
Smew	Rare		Bar-tailed Godwit	W	
Goosander	W		Black-tailed Godwit *(icelandica)*	P, w	
Red-breasted Merganser	W		Turnstone	W, p	
Ruddy Duck	Rare	Irregular	Knot	W	
Red-legged Partridge	All	Regular	Ruff	P	

SPECIES RECORDED (distinctive subspecies in italics)	Occurrence	Breeding Status	SPECIES RECORDED (distinctive subspecies in italics)	Occurrence	Breeding Status
Curlew Sandpiper	P		Grey Heron	All	Regular
Temminck's Stint	Historic		Purple Heron	Historic	
Sanderling	Rare		Great White Egret	Rare	
Dunlin	W, p		Little Egret	All	Regular
Purple Sandpiper	Once		Osprey	P	
Little Stint	P		Honey Buzzard	Rare	
White-rumped Sandpiper	Historic		Sparrowhawk	All	Regular
Pectoral Sandpiper	Historic		Goshawk	Rare	
Long-billed Dowitcher	Historic		Marsh Harrier	All	Possible
Woodcock	W		Hen Harrier	Rare	
Jack Snipe	W		Montagu's Harrier	Once	
(Common) Snipe	W	?Historic	Red Kite	All	Historic
Terek Sandpiper	Once		White-tailed Eagle	Historic	
Wilson's Phalarope	Historic		Common Buzzard	All	Regular
Red-necked Phalarope	Historic		Barn Owl	All	Regular
Grey Phalarope	Once		Little Owl	All	Regular
Common Sandpiper	P		Long-eared Owl	All	Regular
Spotted Sandpiper	Once		Short-eared Owl	W	
Green Sandpiper	P, w		Tawny Owl	All	Regular
Lesser Yellowlegs	Once		Hoopoe	Historic	
(Common) Redshank	P, w	Regular	Kingfisher	All	Regular
Marsh Sandpiper	Once		Bee-eater	Once	
Wood Sandpiper	Rare		Wryneck	Once	Historic
Spotted Redshank	P		Lesser Spotted Woodpecker	All	Irregular
Greenshank	P, w		Great Spotted Woodpecker	All	Regular
Kittiwake	Rare		Green Woodpecker	All	Regular
Black-headed Gull	All	Regular	Kestrel	All	Regular
Little Gull	P		Eleonora's Falcon	Once	
Mediterranean Gull	S, w		Merlin	W	
Common Gull	W		Hobby	S	Possible
Great Black-backed Gull	W		Peregrine (Falcon)	All	
Glaucous Gull	Historic		Ring-necked Parakeet	Rare	Irregular
Herring Gull	All	Regular	Red-backed Shrike	Historic	Historic
Yellow-legged Gull	P		Great Grey Shrike	Once	
Lesser Black-backed Gull	All	Regular	Jay	All	Regular
Caspian Tern	Historic		Magpie	All	Regular
Sandwich Tern	P		Jackdaw	All	Regular
Little Tern	P		Rook	All	Regular
Common Tern	S	Regular	Carrion Crow	All	Regular
Arctic Tern	P		Hooded Crow	Historic	
White-Winged Black Tern	Historic		Raven	Once	Historic
Black Tern	P		Waxwing	Rare	
Great Skua	Once		Coal Tit	All	Regular
Pomarine Skua	Once		Marsh Tit	Once	?Historic
Arctic Skua	Once		Willow Tit	Historic	Historic
Long-tailed Skua	Once		Blue Tit	All	Regular
Little Auk	Rare		Great Tit	All	Regular
Guillemot	Rare		Bearded Tit	All	Irregular
Puffin	Historic		Woodlark	Once	
Red-throated Diver	W		Skylark	All	Regular
Black-throated Diver	Once		Shorelark	Historic	
Great Northern Diver	W		Sand Martin	P	
Leach's Petrel	Historic		(Barn) Swallow	S, p	Regular
Fulmar	Once		House Martin	S, p	Regular
Manx Shearwater	Historic		Red-rumped Swallow	Rare	
White Stork	Once		Cetti's Warbler	All	Regular
Gannet	Rare		Long-tailed Tit	All	Regular
(Great) Cormorant *(carbo)*	All	Regular	Wood Warbler	Historic	
Continental race (sinensis)	All	Regular	Yellow-browed Warbler	Historic	
Shag	Rare		Willow Warbler	S, p	Regular
Glossy Ibis	Rare		Chiffchaff	S, w	Regular
Spoonbill	Once		Sedge Warbler	S	Regular
Bittern	Rare		Reed Warbler	S	Regular
Night Heron	Once		Marsh Warbler	Once	
Cattle Egret	S	Regular	Grasshopper Warbler	Rare	

SPECIES RECORDED (distinctive subspecies in italics)	Occurrence	Breeding Status	SPECIES RECORDED (distinctive subspecies in italics)	Occurrence	Breeding Status
Blackcap	S, w	Regular	Yellow Wagtail *(flavissima)*	P, s	Regular
Garden Warbler	S	Regular	*Blue-headed Wagtail (flava)*	Rare	
Lesser Whitethroat	S	Regular	*Grey-headed Wagtail (thunbergi)*	Historic	
(Common) Whitethroat	S	Regular	Grey Wagtail	All	Regular
Dartford Warbler	Rare		Pied Wagtail *(yarrelli)*	All	Regular
Firecrest	P		*White Wagtail (alba)*	P	
Goldcrest	All	Regular	Richard's Pipit	Historic	
Wren	All	Regular	Meadow Pipit	W, p	Irregular
Nuthatch	All	Irregular	Tree Pipit	Rare	
Treecreeper	All	Regular	Water Pipit	W	
Rose-coloured Starling	Historic		(Scandinavian) Rock Pipit *(littoralis)*	W	
(Common) Starling	All	Regular	Chaffinch	All	Regular
Ring Ouzel	Once		Brambling	W	
Blackbird	All	Regular	Hawfinch	Once	
Fieldfare	W		Bullfinch	All	Regular
Redwing	W		Greenfinch	All	Regular
Song Thrush	All	Regular	Twite	Rare	
Mistle Thrush	All	Regular	Linnet	All	Regular
Spotted Flycatcher	P	Irregular	Common Redpoll	Rare	
Robin	All	Regular	Lesser Redpoll	W	
Nightingale	S	Regular	(Common) Crossbill	Rare	
Pied Flycatcher	Rare		Goldfinch	All	Regular
Black Redstart	All	Irregular	Serin	Once	
(Common) Redstart	Rare		Siskin	W	
Whinchat	P		Lapland Bunting	Historic	
Stonechat	W	Irregular	Snow Bunting	Rare	
(Northern) Wheatear *(oenanthe)*	P		Corn Bunting	All	Regular
Greenland Wheatear (leucorhoa)	Rare		Yellowhammer	All	Regular
House Sparrow	All	Regular	Ortolan Bunting	Historic	
Tree Sparrow	Rare	?Historic	Reed Bunting	All	Regular
Dunnock	All	Regular			

Examples of species seen in the patch that were not in a truly wild state:

Category 'E'- includes escapes from captivity and species without self-sustaining wild populations

Black Swan (family party seen in 2009)
Bar-headed Goose
Ruddy Shelduck (possibly from populations on the continent)
Wood Duck
Chiloe Wigeon
White-cheeked Pintail
Cinnamon Teal
Hottentot Teal
Rosybill

Chilean Flamingo
Harris's Hawk
Red-tailed Hawk
Diamond Dove
Cockatiel
Budgerigar
Peach-faced Lovebird
Zebra Finch
Canary

Explanation of list nomenclature and sequence

In recent years, bird names, and the order in which species are listed, have been in a state of flux, with attempts to standardise them competing with advances in scientific understanding of their genetic relationships.

The order of the species in the above main list is taken from the June 2021 updated version of the 9th edition of the British List as published by the British Ornithologists' Union Records Committee (BOURC). The names used generally follow BOURC conventions though some have been qualified to better reflect current local usage and to try to minimise confusion.

← Large numbers of hirundines pass through our area on their journey north each spring. Here (l to r) a Sand Martin, a House Martin, two Swallow and another Sand Martin stop for a rest at Lofts Farm. Apr 2021 (JB)

↓ Garden Warbler is a scarce local breeder, now best looked for along the Chelmer & Blackwater Navigation.

For a few years, they were regular in Elms Farm Park, where this bird was photographed. Apr 2014 (JB)

↑ Lapwing is a rapidly declining breeding species in the UK but many hundreds still arrive to winter on the estuary and in fields around Maldon. Their striking wing pattern makes them easily recognisable in flight. Nov 2013 (SP)

← Autumn migration is a time to look out for unusual passage birds, such as Little Stint, the world's smallest species of wader. Here is one seen at Heybridge Pits. Oct 2017 (SW)

APPENDIX V

Butterflies Recorded within the Maldon Study Area

Species recorded 2000–2020

Swallowtail *Papilio machaon*	Single record (2012) (possibly European race)
Essex Skipper *Thymelicus lineola*	Resident
Small Skipper *Thymelicus sylvestris*	Resident
Large Skipper *Ochlodes sylvanus*	Resident
Orange-tip *Anthocharis cardamines*	Resident
Large White *Pieris brassicae*	Resident
Small White *Pieris rapae*	Resident
Green-veined White *Pieris napi*	Resident
Clouded Yellow *Colias croceus*	Migrant
Brimstone *Gonepteryx rhamni*	Resident
Wall *Lasiommata megera*	Recent records (2018 & 2019)
Speckled Wood *Pararge aegeria*	Resident
Small Heath *Coenonympha pamphilus*	Resident
Ringlet *Aphantopus hyperantus*	Resident
Meadow Brown *Maniola jurtina*	Resident
Gatekeeper *Pyronia tithonus*	Resident
Marbled White *Melanargia galathea*	Widespread recent records (likely colonist)
Silver-washed Fritillary *Argynnis paphia*	Recent colonist (2019)
White Admiral *Limenitis camilla*	Recent colonist
Purple Emperor *Apatura iris*	Single record in potential breeding location (2019)
Red Admiral *Vanessa atalanta*	Migrant breeder, some probably overwinter
Painted Lady *Vanessa cardui*	Migrant
Peacock *Aglais io*	Resident
Small Tortoiseshell *Aglais urticae*	Resident
Comma *Polygonia c-album*	Resident

Small Copper *Lycaena phlaeas*	Resident
Purple Hairstreak *Favonius quercus*	Resident
Green Hairstreak *Callophrys rubi*	Resident, scarce
White-letter Hairstreak *Satyrium w-album*	Resident, scarce
Holly Blue *Celastrina argiolus*	Resident
Brown Argus *Aricia agestis*	Resident
Common Blue *Polyommatus icarus*	Resident

Recorded just prior to study period:

Camberwell Beauty *Nymphalis antiopa*	Migrant, single record in 1995

Note: Butterfly names and sequence aligned to UKButterflies.co.uk, June 2021

Conservation status

According to 'The Butterfly Red Data List for Great Britain' maintained for the JNCC by Butterfly Conservation (latest edition published in 2010), those of our regular butterflies classified as being of significant conservation concern from a UK context are:

White-letter Hairstreak —	Endangered
White Admiral —	Vulnerable
Small Heath —	Near Threatened

The potential re-colonists Purple Emperor and Wall Brown are both classified as Near Threatened

Historical records

Historically, there was a greater diversity of butterflies in the area. Around the end of the 19th century, there were records of a couple more fritillaries, Pearl-bordered *Boloria euphrosyne* and High Brown *Fabriciana adippe,* as well as Large Tortoiseshell *Nymphalis polychloros,* Grizzled Skipper *Pyrgus malvae,* Brown Hairstreak *Thecia betulae* and Pale Clouded Yellow *Colias hyale*.

Of these, the Pearl-bordered and High Brown Fritillaries survived till the middle of the 20th century (as did the Silver-washed Fritillary). Large Tortoiseshell ended up becoming extinct around 1950 and actually became extinct in the UK.

There is also an isolated Maldon record of Grayling *Hipparchia semele* from 1947.

APPENDIX VI

Notes on Conservation Status of Moths Recorded within the Maldon Study Area

As noted in the main text, moths are a sensitive indicator of the health of our environment. It is important to keep a track of rarer species, not just for their own sake, but also because if they are in trouble it may mean that their habitats are in trouble, impacting other organisms and ecological relationships that as yet we may know little about.

Total number of species recorded 2000–2020

	Butterflies	Macro-moths	Micro-moths	TOTAL
Species recorded 2000-2020 (percentage of total recorded)	32 (3.5%)	424 (46.1%)	463 (50.4%)	**919**

A number of different assessments of moth populations have been made to identify which species need special conservation measures.

Macro-moths

For macro-moths, conservation status is here derived from:

- UK Red List species from Zoë Randle et al., *"Atlas of Britain & Ireland's Larger Moths"*, 2019, using data from 2019 Butterfly Conservation report to English Nature
- UK BAP List, maintained by Butterfly Conservation
- Essex Red List, maintained by Essex Field Club

Total species	UK Red List			Essex Red List	UK BAP
	NT	VU	EN		
424	24	10	3	41	53

Red List Ratings:

NT	Near Threatened
VU	Vulnerable
EN	Endangered
BAP	Subject to a Biodiversity Action Plan

Emperor Moth, the UK's only member of the silk-moth family.
Female, Heybridge, Apr 2020 (SW)

Elephant Hawk-moth, a very attractive species that often occurs in gardens.
Hazeleigh Wood, Oct 2018 (SW)

Micro-moths

Conservation status of micro moths is derived from:

- UK Red List species from *"A review of the status of Microlepidoptera in Britain"*, 2012, Butterfly Conservation
- UK BAP list, maintained by Butterfly Conservation
- Essex Red List, maintained by Essex Field Club

Total species	Status of commoner species		Proposed for UK Red List			Essex Red List species	UK BAP species
	Nationally Scarce B	Nationally Scarce A	pRDB3	pRDB2	pRDB1		
463	44	8	5	1	2	53	1

Nationally scarce B	Occurs in 31-100 10km squares
Nationally scarce A	Occurs in 16-30 10km squares
pRDB3	Occurs in 11-15 10km squares
pRDB2	Occurs in 6-10 10km squares
pRDB3	Occurs in 5 or less 10km squares
BAP	Subject to a Biodiversity Action Plan

APPENDIX VII

Dragonflies Recorded within the Maldon Study Area

Damselflies 2000–2020

Willow Emerald *Chalcolestes viridis*	Recent colonist (first local record 2013)
Scarce Emerald *Lestes dryas*	Resident, scarce
Common Emerald *Lestes sponsa*	Resident
Banded Demoiselle *Calopteryx splendens*	Resident
White-legged *Platycnemis pennipes*	Resident, scarce
Azure *Coenagrion puella*	Resident
Common Blue *Enallagma cyathigerum*	Resident
Red-eyed *Erythromma najas*	Resident
Small Red-eyed *Erythromma viridulum*	Recent colonist
Blue-tailed *Ischnura elegans*	Resident
Large Red *Pyrrhosoma nymphula*	Resident

Dragonflies 2000–2020

Southern Migrant Hawker *Aeshna affinis* (also known as Southern Migrant Hawker)	First records 2020 likely colonist
Southern Hawker *Aeshna cyanea*	Resident
Brown Hawker *Aeshna grandis*	Resident
Migrant Hawker *Aeshna mixta*	Resident, probably boosted by migrants
Emperor *Anax imperator*	Resident
Hairy *Brachytron pratense*	Resident
Broad-bodied Chaser *Libellula depressa*	Resident
Scarce Chaser *Libellula fulva*	Resident, localised
Four-spotted Chaser *Libellula quadrimaculata*	Resident
Black-tailed Skimmer *Orthetrum cancellatum*	Resident
Ruddy Darter *Sympetrum sanguineum*	Resident
Common Darter *Sympetrum striolatum*	Resident

Note: Dragon & Damselfly names and sequence aligned to British Dragonfly Society website, June 2021

Conservation status

According to 'The Odonata Red Data List for Great Britain' maintained for the JNCC by the British Dragonfly Society (latest edition published in 2008), those of our dragonflies and damselflies classified as being of significant conservation concern from a UK context are:

Scarce Emerald Damselfly —   Near Threatened

Scarce Chaser —   Near Threatened

← Sea Club-rush growing along the borrow dyke towards Mundon — this is the key habitat where Scarce Emerald Damselfly has been found locally

→ Scarce Emerald Damselfly, to the east of Mundon Sluice, June 2021 (SW)

APPENDIX VIII

Nature Reserves and other Priority Wildlife Sites in and around Maldon

Blackwater Estuary

The Blackwater Estuary is the one site around Maldon that has received full international recognition for its wildlife value and is covered as a whole by a number of different environmental designations.

On an international level, it is recognised as a UNESCO Ramsar site for its wintering populations of wetland birds, and it is also classified by the UK government as a Special Protection Area under the Wildlife & Countryside Act and 2010 Conservation Regulations. (The Essex estuaries together are a UK Special Area of Conservation).

Flock of Golden Plover wintering on the estuary, Nov 2015 (JB)

Sites of Special Scientific Interest

Sites of Special Scientific Interest (SSSIs) are those sites that have been designated by the government conservation agency (currently Natural England) as being of conservation importance and places specific legal obligations on landowners and planners.

The Blackwater Estuary is the only site within our study area legally designated as an SSSI for its biological value. There are also two SSSI's here that have been designated for their geological merit: Lofts Farm Gravel Pit and Maldon Cutting (lying along the bypass between Spital Road and London Road).

Essex Wildlife Trust Reserves

EWT manage two reserves in our study area:

- Chigborough Lakes
- Maldon Wick

National Trust Properties

- Northey Island (including some of the fields on the south side of the river)

  (Note that currently only pre-arranged visits to the island are allowed)

Local Wildlife Sites

These are sites on a list of areas of wildlife importance created by the Maldon Nature Conservation Study that was carried out by Essex Ecology Services (EECOS) at the behest of Maldon District Council. The list is currently maintained by the Essex Wildlife Trust Biological Records Centre.

Chapmans bridge and the canal at Elms Farm Park

Note that this listing does not directly confer any level of protection however it is a requirement of Maldon's District Design Guide and associated Landscape and Green Infrastructure Technical Document (Dec 2017) that would-be developers must take them into account when evaluating the environmental impacts of any proposals.

The Local Wildlife Sites that fall within the area covered by this book are listed below.

	Grid reference
Ma1 River Chelmer	TL790093 to 838082
Ma18 Kent Wood	TL824030
Ma19 Parsonage Wood	TL824047
Ma21 Wood Corner Grove	TL829060
Ma22 Bog Wood	TL829068
Ma24 Hazeleigh Hall Wood	TL834042
Ma25 Blackwater Rail Trail	TL849080
Ma28 Howe Wood (overlaps edge of study area)	TL837012
Ma29 Langford Churchyard	TL837090
Ma31 Langford Cut Meadows	TL838087
Ma33 Rookery Grove	TL840025
Ma34 Farther Howe Green	TL842012
Ma35 Maldon Wick (the EWT reserve)	TL842057
Ma36 River Chelmer Beeleigh to Fullbridge	TL842077
Ma39 Hilly Fields	TL845074
Ma40 Elms Farm Park	TL846079
Ma41 Ironworks Meadow	TL847076
Ma46 Middle Wood (overlaps edge of study area)	TL854101
Ma49 Heybridge Wood	TL856090
Ma50 Heybridge Creek	TL857077
Ma55 South Wood (overlaps edge of study area)	TL862104
Ma57 Heybridge Gravel Pit	TL865070
Ma59 Mundon Furze	TL869023
Ma60 Limbourne Creek	TL869049
Ma63 Chigborough Lakes (including the EWT reserve area plus also Lofts Farm and some lakes to the south)	TL877086
Ma64 Mundon Oaks	TL881026

Local Nature Reserves

Local Nature Reserves (LNRs) are a statutory designation made by principal local authorities for sites with wildlife or geological features that are of special interest locally.

At the time of writing, none of the above identified Local Wildlife Sites (or indeed any other) are designated as Local Nature Reserves by Maldon District Council.

Thus there is currently an absence of local legislation to specifically protect any of the key sites for wildlife within the Maldon area.

Traditional charcoal burning being carried out in Hazeleigh Wood

INDEX

Includes all entries in the main text of the book (excluding Appendices)

BIRDS	FISH	GENERAL (People, Places, Events, Activities etc)
MAMMALS	INVERTEBRATES	
REPTILES & AMPHIBIANS	PLANTS & FUNGI	

Some more of Maldon's diverse array of insects

Great Red Sedge, Hazeleigh, June 2018 (SW) This is the UK's largest Caddis Fly and is a popular choice for reproducing as a fly-tied lure for fishermen angling for trout.

Tree Bumblebee, Lofts Farm, July 2021 (JB). Insects perform an essential role as pollinators.While bees are well known for this, the actions of wasps and hoverflies, amongst others, are also vital.

False Ladybird, Hazeleigh Wood, Aug 2019 (SW). In a classic form of deception, this small beetle mimics ladybirds in an attempt to deter predators.

Roesel's Bush-cricket, Southey Creek, July 2021 (SW). Steadily increasing during the study period, this species is now readily found along the sea wall during the summer.

Rose Chafer, Chigborough Lakes, July 2021 (SW). Another attractive species. As its name suggests, best looked for when roses are flowering.

Rhyncites auratus, Chigborough Lakes, May 2015 (SW) This is one of only a handful of sites in the UK where this currently rare iridescent weevil has been recorded.

BIRDS	FISH	GENERAL (People, Places,
MAMMALS	INVERTEBRATES	Events, Activities etc)
REPTILES & AMPHIBIANS	PLANTS & FUNGI	

BIRDS	FISH	GENERAL (People, Places, Events, Activities etc)
MAMMALS	INVERTEBRATES	
REPTILES & AMPHIBIANS	PLANTS & FUNGI	

BIRDS	FISH	GENERAL (People, Places, Events, Activities etc)
MAMMALS	INVERTEBRATES	
REPTILES & AMPHIBIANS	PLANTS & FUNGI	

Some more views from around the Maldon Study Area

Mundon Oaks
Maldon Town from Heybridge Pits
The Chelmer & Blackwater Navigation

Estuary view at sunset
The estuary from 'The Dump'
The route of the old railway line at Maldon Wick

Brent Geese, Blackwater Estuary, Nov 2012 (SW)

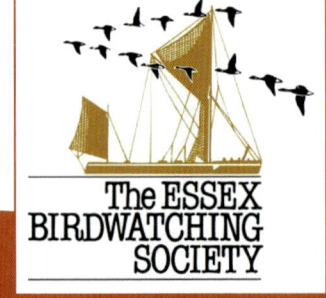